Pure & Beautiful
VEGAN COOKING

First published in 2016 by
Page Street Publishing Co.
27 Congress Street, Suite 103
Salem, MA 01970
www.pagestreetpublishing.com

Distributed by Macmillan, sales in Canada by The Canadian Manda Group.

19 18 17 16 1 2 3 4 5

ISBN-13: 978-1-62414-199-7
ISBN-10: 1-62414-199-4

Library of Congress Control Number: 2015954407

Cover and book design by Page Street Publishing Co.
Photography by Kathleen Henry

Printed and bound in China

Page Street is proud to be a member of 1% for the Planet. Members donate one percent of their sales to one or more of the over 1,500 environmental and sustainability charities across the globe who participate in this program.

Pure & Beautiful Vegan Cooking

RECIPES INSPIRED BY RURAL LIFE IN **ALASKA**

Kathleen Henry

writer and photographer of
the vegan food blog Produce On Parade

contents

mornings

afternoons

evenings

both fuss-free and leisurely crafted meals 65

snacks, sides & salads

rumbling stomach quellers, meal copilots and crowd pleasers 109

bakery

sweets

drinks

dedication

Todd—My loving husband. We ventured forth on our vegan adventure due to your rheumatoid arthritis. It's unbelievable how healthy you've become since implementing a plant-based diet, free from meat, eggs and dairy. Who could have imagined that veganism would be such a huge part of our lives? I want to thank you for beseeching me to start a food blog; an idea that took *several* years of convincing before I finally conceded. You've always advocated my talents and have been my cornerstone throughout this vegan *enlightenment*. Always encouraging, always aiding, always patient and always so willing to try new foods and the recipes I develop (even when copious amounts of beets are involved). My true love, *thank you*.

Family & Friends—You've always been so eager to accommodate Todd and I in our new lifestyle: Habitually offering vegan versions of dishes, ensuring that we *always* had something to eat and being so incredibly supportive to us both. I'm awed by all that you do and how much love you have in your hearts. We're so lucky to have such benevolent, loving and thoughtful family and friends, *thank you*.

Produce On Parade Readers—Without you, none of this would be possible. You've been with Todd, Bailey and I on our Alaskan adventures through uncharted vegan territory since 2013. The online community at Produce On Parade is such an inspiration and a beautiful support system for me. You've showed me that caring too much or having too much empathy is *never* a flaw and should be celebrated. I've discovered so many friends and like-minded fellows in this bright and beautiful, tight-knit group. You all mean the world to me. Thank you for your unwavering encouragement and praise throughout the years.

All Sentient Beings—I hope this cookbook blooms compassion in the heart of the cook. All living creatures, from a human being to a wee mouse, deserve to lead happy and peaceful lives free from suffering. I hope one day we can achieve this; it seems as though we're moving in the right direction.

I read you're supposed to dedicate your book to only one or two people; otherwise you risk lessening the *specialness* of such an honor as that of a book dedication. *Whatevs*. You are *all* my champions and I don't know where I would be in this world without such kind and loving people to encourage me, inspire me and support me. Thank you, from the deepest corner of my heart.

"The world is indeed full of peril, and in it there are many dark places; but still there is much that is fair,

and though in all lands love is now mingled with grief, it grows perhaps the greater."

—J.R.R. Tolkien

introduction

I was born and raised in the small, rural town of Palmer, Alaska. Growing up on a mountainside in the fertile, agricultural belt of Alaska, I spent my childhood outside in nature. Padding playfully down our driveway and across the dirt road, I'd wind my way through the forest trail to my grandparent's home, a short half mile away.

My grandparents weren't farmers, but you wouldn't have known it. Cabbage, potatoes, broccoli, peas, carrots, asparagus, even corn, were among some of the vegetables that I remember plucking and munching on. My grandma showed me how to use the giant rhubarb leaf as a hat when it was raining out, warning me not to eat the leaves, as they are poisonous. In the summer we'd harvest huge, plump Canby raspberries as well as the smaller, sweeter variety. There were the most delicious strawberries you've ever eaten, and even juicy currents. My brothers and I would spend our summer days picking raspberries, rows upon rows of the little jewels. We would seek shade and sneak a break whenever we could, hidden in the never-ending tangles and thorns.

This wasn't a little garden, no; this was a monster of a thing. And it *all* had to be picked. This was my introduction to fruits and vegetables. However, my diet wasn't vegan. Far from it, because in the wilderness of Alaska I grew up eating moose, caribou, rabbit, grouse, salmon, halibut and pickled pike. Most food, especially fresh fruits and vegetables, has to be transported up to Alaska and that makes it expensive. Many folks up here do a lot of hunting and fishing to help them subsist, filling up their deep storage freezers to the brim for winter. Many families live on game meat and fish alone, as opposed to buying store-bought meats. My dad likes to joke that when my brothers and I first had a "beef" hamburger (as opposed to a moose hamburger), we exclaimed that it was the best hamburger we'd ever eaten and wondered why it tasted so good. Except it was never really a joke . . . we had never eaten beef! Such is the life of a native Alaskan.

I'm not unaware of the fact that Alaska and veganism don't necessarily go hand in hand. The Last Frontier is bountiful in wild animals . . . that people often kill for meat. Not to mention that the harsh winters and short growing season don't really allow the state to teem with a steady abundance of fruits and vegetables like others do. We don't have a Trader Joe's or a Whole Foods Market and the entire state has only one Costco—in Anchorage, a 50–mile drive from where I live. Many people already view veganism as an expensive way to eat, now imagine being vegan in *Alaska*, where things are already so expensive! However, I am here to tell you that it can be done beautifully and it's not in the least more expensive than a traditional carnivorous diet.

I obtain most of my produce from Full Circle, an organic community-supported agriculture (CSA) cooperative that the Northwestern states participate in and that carries Alaskan-grown produce. This is where I acquire most my fruit (nonberry related), like apples, peaches and plums. Also, farmer's markets and our grocery stores carry local broccoli, potatoes, carrots and other vegetables. This is where, when in season, I acquire most of my vegetables. Nuts, seeds, pantry items and vegan alternatives to cream cheese, sour cream and so on. I purchase from our local Fred Meyer and Safeway grocery stores. More elusive items that I find necessary in my vegan kitchen, such as kombu, agar agar powder, matcha and so forth I find online at Amazon and Vitacost.

There can still be a plethora of healthy, vegan food options even if you live in a quaint, rural Alaskan town and happen to be vegan. All it takes is a little know-how and some culinary skills. If I can make my way being vegan with seemingly limited ingredients way up here in the Last Frontier, then I know you can, too. One doesn't have to be next door to a specialty health food store or have a pantry full of odd ingredients. This is great *accessible* vegan food.

However, having limitations can be good. It challenges me, makes me think outside the norm, makes me more *creative*. It makes me craft something better, something new, something *unique*. I hope to share that with you through this cookbook. To me, there's an immense importance in cultivating a life filled with *real* and healthy cooking, a respect for nature, gardening, reading, joy, reflection, serenity, friendship, a healthy family life and the ability to repair things as opposed to giving up. Some of these ideas seem so far away in many of our lives; maybe not all the time, but *sometimes*. I feel it too, but so much less so since adopting a vegan lifestyle.

Veganism has fostered a sense of community and compassion for not only the other creatures that roam this earth with us, but for the people around me as well. It's made me keen on every one of my actions. Each step I take is a little lighter and friendlier towards the planet; I recycle more, buy cruelty-free products, use up each scrap of food, don't buy more than I need and live a simpler and more peaceful life. I'm friendlier, have more confidence, realize that we are all connected and have a new appreciation for the world around me and the miracle of its orchestration. This may sound like the murmurs of a wandering shaman—I get that. There's no bigger skeptic than me, but could a small step of simply switching to veggie burgers from cow hamburgers change your world? It did for Todd and me. I invite you to try a few of these recipes, eat fewer animals, muster up some compassion, embrace a bit of change and fire up your taste buds!

Katie Sferry

quick tips on ingredients & equipment

Hey, you! Give this little section a quick glance through. It's short and sweet and will answer any questions you may have regarding some of the ingredients and/or equipment used in this cookbook. Whilst flipping through a vegan cookbook, one can plainly see that we plant-based folks sometimes incorporate some pretty perplexing stuff into our meals. Like *nooch*. Nope, not a dirty word. It's just a nickname for nutritional yeast!

Are you asking yourself if you *really* need to purchase a cast-iron skillet? I mean, who needs one more kitchen gadget just loitering around in a busy cupboard! And vegan cheese . . . where to even start? Does it even come in slices? I don't like to take supplements, but there is one that vegans should not go without. Do you know which? Never fear, all these questions are answered along with a few tips you may not know!

PANTRY

Agar Agar - This powdery substance derived from seaweed is a gelling agent that comes in flakes as well as a powder. I recommend using the powder as oftentimes the flakes can leave a granular feel in some dishes. You'll also need to use much less of the powder than of the flakes. I use agar agar in place of gelatin in equal amounts. It can be found online at Amazon.com and in health food stores.

Coconut Oil - I like to use unrefined (virgin) coconut oil in most of my recipes because I favor its pronounced coconut flavor. However, if you are partial to a more neutral flavor, use refined coconut oil. The latter also has a higher smoke point than the unrefined version. Use whichever you prefer.

Flaxseed - I buy whole flaxseed and use a spare coffee grinder (the same one I use for spices) to grind it myself. Ground flaxseed doesn't keep as well as whole flaxseeds, so it's best to grind it yourself. I usually grind a small jar's worth to have on hand. It just takes a minute and this way I don't have to grind some up each time I need it. However, preground flaxseed can be purchased as well if you're not inclined to grind your own. Keep the whole and ground flaxseed stored in the fridge.

Kala Namak - This sulfurous salt can be found online at Amazon.com. It's one of those specialty food items that I'll only use for a few things (which I detest purchasing), however, if you find yourself making my Spot-On Scrambled "Eggs" (page 24) or need an "eggy" flavor in a dish, the stuff is *absolutely* essential.

Miso Paste - There are several different kinds of miso paste that vary in color and flavor intensity. Red miso paste is the most robust and flavorful, followed by yellow miso and then the subtle white miso. I prefer red miso because I like its stronger taste. However, feel free to use your favorite, and if you're new to miso perhaps start by trying yellow or white first.

Nutritional Yeast - This stuff is my crack. Affectionately coined *nooch*, it's a great addition to dishes that require a cheesy flavor. It's grown on molasses and packed with protein and B_{12}, a vitamin that vegans need to supplement in their diet (see below). Find it in the bulk section of your local grocery store. Nutritional yeast is *not* the same as nor interchangeable with brewers or bakers yeast. It can be purchased as small flakes or large flakes (my preference) and is as bright as a yellow slicker! I prefer the large flakes as I find them more suitable for topping toast; the small flakes tend to collect on the roof of my mouth.

Soy Sauce - A fantastic alternative to regular ol' salt in many dishes, it lends that "umami" flavor, which can be hard to get from a vegan diet. Just use a splash of soy sauce in savory dishes in place of salt. You can do the same with miso as well.

Sugar - Sugar is often manufactured using a filtering agent that helps decolorize it. A common agent is bone char, which is derived from the bones of cattle. White sugar, powdered sugar and even brown sugar can all be manufactured using it. Super creepy, right? To avoid perpetuating the use of bone char, choose organic brands, which cannot by law be filtered using the stuff.

Wine - Many wines are clarified with nonvegan fining agents such as milk proteins, egg whites, gelatin and even a type of protein made from fish bladders. *Say whaaa?* Yep, pretty freakin' weird. There are vegan alternative agents though; a type of clay known as bentonite as well as activated charcoal. Some winemakers are even leaving their wines unfiltered, thus making fining agents obsolete. Occasionally I'll find bottles labeled as vegan and many organic wines *are* vegan, but if you really want to be sure, I would recommend checking the website Barnivore.com. It comprises an extensive list of alcoholic beverages that are denoted as vegan or not-vegan, along with correspondence from the manufacturers for verification. The website is free and there's even a Barnivore app for smartphones for $1.99. I use it all the time.

Xanthan Gum - This powdery, white substance is actually gel derived from a special kind of bacteria that develops on sugar. The gel is dried and ground to make xanthan gum, which is used as a thickener and emulsifier. I add the stuff to baked goods, custards, puddings and smoothies to create a super creamy texture. It's a hero when blended into green smoothies; they go from watery and separated to thick and creamy! Xanthan gum can be found at your local grocery store or online at Vitacost.com and Amazon.com.

VEGAN DAIRY

Butter - Comes in a few different varieties, namely the stick kind (yep, just like regular ol' butter) and the spreadable kind that comes in a small tub. I've used both in baking and they do act differently, so I strongly advise using only the stick butter when it comes to baking. I buy the spreadable stuff only because of Todd's addiction to toast. Both versions should be readily available at your local grocery store. We like the brand Earth Balance.

Cheese - Vegan cheese comes in all shapes and sizes, and can be made from a wide assortment of plant-based ingredients. There are two main categories of vegan cheese: cheese made from nuts and seeds, and those made from soy-based ingredients. The first can be soft, hard or even grate-able and melt-able. This cheese is made from nuts and seeds and/or their milk. Preshredded cheeses are generally made from soy as well as many of the presliced, meltable cheeses. With so many to choose from, it's not hard to find a favorite. We recommend Daiya shredded cheese when needed, Tofutti sliced cheese for its meltability and Field Roast's Chaos cheese (best tasting) which can be found at Whole Foods. It's perfect for things like sandwiches and burgers, or just eating plain! I actually order the Chaos online through my CSA provider, Full Circle, which serves the Northwest.

There are many soft, fancy vegan cheeses that are great for entertaining. These are generally found at natural food stores and might be difficult to acquire at your local grocery store. I confess to hoarding them on vacations when we take our *required* trip to Whole Foods. Alaska doesn't have a Whole Foods Market or Trader Joe's, so they're like Disney World for me! I love perusing all their unique food items.

Sour Cream - Tastes just like regular sour cream made with cow's milk only without all that nasty business of cholesterol and animal cruelty. I recommend the brand Tofutti. No one will know the difference and it should be available at your local grocery store.

Cream Cheese - There are a few different brands available, however, none replicate traditional cream cheese with any excellence. At first I hated the cream cheese by Tofutti, but now I vastly prefer it (or maybe I've forgotten what traditional cream cheeses tastes like!). I've also used the Follow Your Heart and Daiya brands, but with mixed results. Try out a few different brands to find which one you like best.

Mayonnaise - All the vegan mayos I have tried have been wonderful. I prefer the Just Mayo brand and in a close second is the Follow Your Heart brand. I've read that Just Mayo is even available at Wal-Mart! It sneakily sits next to the conventional mayos in the nonrefrigerated condiment section of your grocery store, while Follow Your Heart can be found in the refrigerated section by the vegan cheeses and meat alternatives. Just Mayo is such a perfect replication that it's even fooled my family!

Milk - Switching from cow's milk is the easiest vegan substitution anybody can implement. Various plant milks are available *everywhere* from the refrigerated section to the nonrefrigerated section, to coffee creamers and even little cartons for lunches, straws included. There are so many different kinds available to choose from! Oat, hemp, rice, coconut, flaxseed, soy and every nut and seed imaginable can be rendered into a delicious cow-milk alternative. I primarily use coconut milk or soy milk, and always buy the unsweetened, plain version (as opposed to sweetened or flavored), which is the most adaptable for use in savory dishes. Almond milk can taste a bit off when heated, but it's great for drinking or use in cereal. There are several vanilla and chocolate varieties of almond and soy milk that are absolutely delicious. Also, nut milks are very easy to make at home—all you need is a nut bag or cheesecloth and a blender!

Canned Coconut Milk - The quality of canned coconut milk varies wildly. Don't bother with the "lite" version; it's just watered down. If you prefer, use half a can of the full-fat variety and add half a can of water to your recipe. A frugal tip! Find a quality brand in which the cream separates from the milk in the can. I like to buy the Thai Kitchen brand (red and black can). The stuff is great as an alternative to heavy cream and creates a fabulous whipped cream. Before opening, give the can a good shake to mix the cream and the milk. If you see just *coconut milk* listed as an ingredient in this book, I'm referring to the carton coconut milk found among soy and almond milk, not the canned variety.

EQUIPMENT

Cast Iron Skillet - Confession: I didn't have a large cast iron skillet until about a year ago. It was one of those kitchen items I thought I'd use for just a few meals. I was convinced it would sorrowfully live its days trapped at the bottom of my stack of regular frying pans; an outcast. I *finally* ended up buying this beautiful enameled one I had been eyeing when it went on sale and now I cannot imagine my kitchen without it! I haven't so much as *touched* another frying pan since. The heavy skillet has made its *permanent* home on my cooktop.

Cast iron skillets are pretty inexpensive, at around $25 for a 12-incher (30-cm). They also infuse food with iron (surprise!), which is especially important for vegans and vegetarians who abstain from consuming animals. If you don't have a cast iron skillet, never fear, a regular frying pan or skillet will usually work fine unless otherwise noted. Do take note though that some regular frying pans are not oven-approved, unlike a cast iron skillet. Also, when using a regular frying pan to caramelize onions or fry veggie burgers and the like, the pan can turn black and smoke due to the lengthy cooking times. It's preferable to use a cast iron skillet in these instances.

High-Powered Blender - I know not everyone has the luxury of having a high-speed blender. They can be expensive and I'm really not sure Todd and I would have one if it was not a gift from my mom for our wedding (pre-vegan days even). Now that we're vegan, I cannot imagine living without it. It's almost essential for blending up all kinds of kooky things we vegans like to use as substitutes—I'm looking at you, cashews.

Vegans tend to have a penchant for making their own nut butters and plant milk (among many other things, like the Vegan Queso [page 117] in this book), all of which are made *infinitely* easier with a high-powered, badass blender. However, that's not to say it can't be done with a regular blender or food processor. It just means that nuts will have to be soaked (many people do this anyway), dates will have to be very soft or soaked, and some recipes might take a bit longer to make. I use a Vitamix, but a Blendtec is comparable.

Food Processor - But Katie, don't you have a Vitamix? Yep. I know, I *totally* dragged my feet at buying one when we already had a fancy blender, but I am so super happy we have one. A food processor is just simply *better* at some things and I'd rather shell out a little bit of money than rip my hair out trying to make coconut butter, nut butters, pesto, "tuna" salad and vegan brownies in my blender. If you cook a lot and you can swing it, I highly recommend one.

Silpat (non-stick silicone baking mats) - Like parchment paper, but re-useable! Nothing sticks to these bad boys. Just wash them with warm water when you're done. You can find them in your grocery store kitchen equipment aisle or online. Use them for both savory and sweet items and whenever you'd normally line a pan with parchment.

SUPPLEMENTS

B_{12} - Vegans *do* need to supplement with B_{12}. It's the one exception. However, many people think they'll need a vast array of vitamins when transitioning to a vegan diet. Yet if one consumes a well-rounded, plant-based diet that simply isn't true. Why do vegans need B_{12}? It's formed by a decomposing microbe. If we were vegan 50–100 years ago we'd maybe get enough of the stuff from our vegetables because it's present in dirt. Nowadays though, our veggies are just too well cleaned and waxed; not a speck of dirt on them (in conventional grocery stores anyway). This bacterium grows in the digestion system of animals, so meat-eaters usually have no trouble getting enough . . . but we don't need to resort to that.

Just pick up a bottle of 2,500 mcg sublingual (it's not absorbed through our gut very efficiently, so be sure to get the sublingual kind) and pop it under your tongue once per week. That's it! It's easily found at your local grocery store. It's dirt-cheap and it's impossible to take too much of the stuff because it has a very low toxicity and is a water-soluble vitamin. This means that any excess B_{12} simply exits the body (this is why overloading on nooch results in neon-colored urine). A B_{12} deficiency can be life-threatening, so don't think you can escape this supplement. Plus, with its tasty cherry flavor it's much more appealing than eating dirt anyway . . . or our furry friends!

mornings

recipes for both cover dwellers and enthusiastic risers

Do you fancy yourself a morning person? I wouldn't subscribe myself to that exact breed. Mornings are for silent snuggle sessions and hot tea, in my opinion. I first deduced that I wasn't an "early bird" in high school. As I drearily shuffled my way to the kitchen to prepare my lunch for school, my dad would have already been awake for quite some time. He'd have read the entire newspaper and would be cheerfully making his way out the door as he himself was on his way to high school, as a physics teacher. I remember my dad was always so conversational and unusually sunny. It bothered me. It was all I could do to grunt abridged replies at his merry banter while staring at him, bleary-eyed and pondering how someone could *possibly* have the energy.

Such morning haze extends itself to breakfast as well. I confess I've never been a breakfast eater with any regularity. My sensitive tummy just refuses to welcome food before my mind has had time to fully rouse itself from the fog of sleep; which is certainly longer than one would think . . . or *hope*. No, lunch will do just fine, thank you. A cup o' tea will do me. Personally, conventional breakfast foods are destined to forever be tied to a dish that's wretchedly over-sweet or disgustingly greasy; specifically crafted for a time-frame in which I'd much rather be nestled in the harbor of covers and fluffy pillows, perhaps with a good book, hiding from the unavoidable events of the day.

The selection of breakfast foods to follow have been carefully developed and curated for folks who are both similar to myself (cover dwellers) and similar to my dad (enthusiastic risers). If you're looking for something quick, my Alaskan Muesli (page 23) will be just the thing. Need a sweet treat? Both the Pan-Fried Polenta Cakelets w/ Caramelized Rhubarb Rum Sauce (page 32) and the Vanilla French Toast w/ Maple Roasted Strawberries (page 28) will be wonderful. If a savory breakfast is more appealing, try your hand at one of Todd's favorites, the Tofu Veggie Scramble w/ Roasted Potatoes (page 31) or the nutritious Savory Steel Cut Oats w/ Fava Beans, Sweet Potatoes & Baby Kale (page 27). There's something here for everyone.

caramel banana-oat pancakes

I'm not really a breakfast person but there's nothing quite like a hearty oat pancake, in my opinion. They're one of my favorite breakfast foods!

Drizzled with a date caramel sauce, these pancakes really take breakfast to a whole new level! These guilt-free pancakes and caramel sauce have no added sweeteners or syrups and the pancakes are oil-free. A wonderfully wholesome and nutritious yet decadent and inexpensive breakfast, this makes a terrific treat for a relaxing weekend morning.

serves 2-3

Caramel

5 (90 g) soft medjool dates, pitted (see note)

¾ cups (180 ml) plain, unsweetened nondairy milk, plus more if needed

2 tbsp (30 ml) refined or unrefined coconut oil, melted

Dash of kosher salt

Pancakes

1 tbsp (7 g) ground flaxseed

¾ cup (180 ml) plain, unsweetened non-dairy milk

½ cup (60 g) all-purpose flour

1 tsp baking powder

1 tsp vanilla extract

½ tsp baking soda

¼ tsp kosher salt

1 (120 g) peeled banana, halved and divided

½ cup (50 g) old-fashioned oats, divided

In a blender, blitz all the caramel ingredients until very smooth. Transfer to a small saucepan and bring to a simmer over medium-low heat, whisking occasionally. Allow to gently boil for about 5 minutes, whisking occasionally, until the caramel has darkened slightly. Remove from heat and set aside. Add 1 tablespoon (15 ml) of additional milk at a time to obtain desired viscosity, if needed. Pour into a small pitcher.

Add all the pancake ingredients to a food processor or blender, excluding half of the banana and ¼ cup (25 g) oats. Process until smooth, then stir in the remaining oats. Slice the remaining half of the banana and set aside.

Coat a cast iron skillet (or griddle) with a nonstick cooking spray and heat over medium. Making one pancake at a time, pour the batter onto the skillet using a ¼ cup (60 ml) of the batter. The pancake is ready to flip when the top begins to form bubbles, the batter has set slightly and the underside has browned. Flip and brown on the other side. Repeat with the remainder of the batter.

Serve drizzled with the caramel sauce and top with the sliced banana.

notes: If your dates are a little old and aren't very soft anymore, heat the milk and soak the dates in it for about 10 minutes prior to blending. Medjool dates can be found at your local grocery store and Costco.

If there's extra caramel, it can be stored in the fridge. Dip apples into it or spread onto cinnamon toast for a healthy treat!

alaskan muesli

My husband, Todd, calls muesli "breakfast trail mix." Why pay for overpriced, store-bought muesli when it's so easy and inexpensive to make yourself? Also, you can suit the muesli to your personal taste preferences when making it at home. Raisins (blech!)—I'm looking at you!

This Alaskan muesli stars dried blueberries and a drizzling of Alaskan birch syrup from trees we tap ourselves! If Alaskan birch syrup doesn't present itself to you, maple syrup works great. Muesli is a really healthy and fulfilling way to start any morning—full of fruit, seeds and nuts! I always feel better when I include it as a staple in my diet. This recipe was created for my dad, a.k.a., the Connoisseur of Muesli.

serves 4 / makes 4 ½ cups (519 g) total

2 cups (165 g) old-fashioned oats, dry

½ cup (85 g) dried blueberries (or raisins, cranberries, etc.)

4 (80 g) dried Calimyrna figs, chopped (see note, or use dried dates, apricots, mangoes, etc.)

¼ cup (28 g) ground flaxseed

¼ cup (35 g) sunflower seeds

¼ cup (37 g) pumpkin seeds

¼ cup (28 g) walnuts, chopped

¼ cup (35 g) almonds, chopped

2 tbsp (19 g) sesame seeds

Serve with

Nondairy milk or yogurt

Fresh fruit (bananas, pears, apples, strawberries, etc.)

Drizzling of birch or maple syrup (optional)

Place all the ingredients in a large bowl and stir well to combine. Break apart any of the chopped figs that stick together. Once they are coated in the oat dustings, they won't stick any longer.

Serve with nondairy milk or yogurt and a topping of fresh fruit with a drizzle of syrup, if desired. Alternatively, soak a serving of muesli overnight in milk, in the fridge for cold porridge on the run!

Store in a large air-tight jar or container. Consume within a few weeks.

notes: I buy large bags of Calimyrna figs from Costco. They are like candy!

Feel free to swap out any fruits and/or nuts you like! This muesli is very customizable.

spot-on scrambled "eggs"

My husband is a self-described "egg man." Eggs are his thing. When we went vegan, he sorrowfully accepted the fact that he would never savor the taste of his beloved scrambled eggs again. After a year, it was something he had come to terms with. However, I am happy to tell you that he was wrong! *Sorta.*

It's true, there are no chicken eggs being cracked in our kitchen, but I've developed a scrambled tofu recipe that will rock your egg-lovin' world. Thinly sliced tofu (as opposed to crumbled tofu), yields that *fluffy* scrambled texture, and an eggy, sulfurous black salt are what make this vegan scrambled "egg" recipe stand out from the crowd.

Try it for yourself and see just how akin they are to the real deal! In fact, this recipe mimics eggs so precisely that I pretty much make it exclusively for Todd. I can't really eat it! Eggs are *not* my thing, but if eggs are *your* thing—you're in luck. Pair these with the Scallion and Garlic Steamed Buns (page 35), Skillet Green Beans & Roasted Potatoes (page 122), Nordic Seeded Crispbread (page 144) or Sweet Potato & Hard Apple Cider Bagels (page 155) for a wholesome, vegan breakfast.

serves 4

Tofu

½ tbsp (9 g) vegan stick butter

12 oz (340 g) firm tofu, drained

Seasoning

½ tsp ground turmeric

½ tsp Kala Namak salt or kosher salt

Scant ¼ tsp chili powder

Scant ¼ tsp paprika

¼ tsp ground black pepper

2 tbsp (11 g) nutritional yeast

In a large saucepan, melt the butter over medium-low heat.

Drain the tofu; there's no need to press it as a bit of water is ideal for this recipe. Slice the tofu thinly, about ¼-inch (6-mm) thick, and stir into the saucepan. It's okay if they crumble.

In a small bowl, whisk together the seasoning ingredients and add to the tofu. Stir gently to combine. Cover and cook for about 10 minutes over low to medium-low heat. Remove from heat and stir in the nutritional yeast.

Serve hot and however you like your "eggs"! Todd's tip is to sprinkle a little bit of the Kala Namak salt on top of the tofu for a more robust "eggy" flavor.

savory steel cut oats w/ fava beans, sweet potatoes & baby kale

I feel comfortable describing myself as "not a morning person." This drearily extends itself to breakfast, too. I generally don't eat the stuff; yes I know how taboo this is. Breaking my fast in the morning just doesn't agree with my sometimes sensitive tummy, it seems. And it's no secret that I generally find breakfast foods to be cloying sweet (Belgian waffles), overly greasy (hash browns) or unimaginably monotonous (cold cereal).

That being said, I would be happier than a chickadee to eat this breakfast dish with routine. Cheesy, porridge-like steel cut oats are cooked until tender but still retaining a little bite. The chewy oats mingle with fresh baby kale, and snuggle up to nutty fava beans and steamed sweet potato. Todd and I enjoy this dish with a bit of salsa on the side. What a scrumptious and healthy way to start the day off right!

serves 2-3

2 cups (475 ml) water

2 cups (475 ml) vegetable broth

1 cup (172 g) steel-cut oats, dry

¾ cup (102 g) fava beans (see note)

1 small (272 g) sweet potato, diced

3 tbsp (17 g) large-flake nutritional yeast

¼ tsp ground turmeric

¼ tsp garlic powder

¼ tsp paprika

Dash of ground black pepper

2 cups (33 g) fresh baby kale or spinach

1 (9 g) green onion, sliced on the diagonal

Salsa, for serving (optional)

In a medium saucepan, bring the water and vegetable broth to a boil over high heat. Stir in the oats and bring back to a boil. Reduce to a simmer and cook, uncovered, for about 30 minutes; stirring occasionally. It should bubble gently during this time and the consistency will end up porridge-like. The oats should be tender but still a bit chewy when done.

While the oats cook, bring a small pot of salted water to boil for fava beans. Remove the beans from their large pods and add to the boiling water. Boil for about 5 minutes then rinse under cold water and simply slip off the whitish bean casing with your fingers to compost along with the pods. Set the beans aside.

Steam the diced sweet potato for about 15 minutes, until fork-tender, and set aside. Whisk the nutritional yeast and remaining spices together in a small bowl.

When the oats are done, stir in the spice mixture until well incorporated; then stir in the baby kale.

To serve, divide the oats between 2 or 3 bowls and top with the blanched fava beans, steamed sweet potato, green onion and a bit of salsa.

note: Fava beans are a wonderful treat but they do have to be shelled, boiled and then shelled again. If you're still a bit too sleepy to do all this, feel free to substitute lima beans. They're available in the freezer section and can be zapped in the microwave or boiled prior to use.

vanilla french toast w/ maple roasted strawberries

French toast is one of the only stereotypical breakfast foods that I really enjoy. I'm pretty sure it's because French toast is just a dessert masquerading as a "great way to start the day!" But what do I know? Actually, as it turns out, how to make the most *amazing* French toast!

I am a French-toast-maker extraordinaire, there's no sense in being humble about it. I learned how to make the most splendid and lavish French toast you ever did eat when I worked as a cook for the Hatcher Pass Lodge. The little A-frame is *still* run by the long-time owner/resident and vegetarian (he introduced me to tempeh) Bostonian. The most important thing I learned from him, regarding French toast, was that one does not make it with regular ol' sandwich bread. If you're doing that, you *must* stop. I forbid it. *Absolutely dreadful stuff.* French toast made with actual french bread is an *entirely* different experience. My French toast is infused with vanilla and smothered in a roasted strawberry sauce for a decadent and satisfying start to the day.

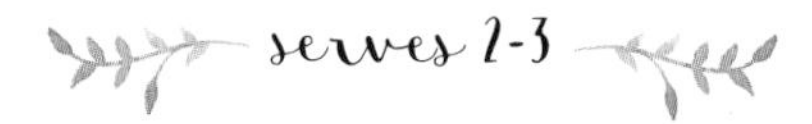

Sauce

3 cups (466 g) fresh strawberries, hulled and quartered

¼ cup (60 ml) maple syrup

½ tbsp (7 ml) fresh lemon juice

Dash of ground black pepper

Toast

6–9 (1-inch [2.5-cm]) thick slices of French bread, a few days old if possible (see note)

1 cup (240 ml) nondairy milk

2 tbsp (18 g) all-purpose flour

1 tbsp (15 ml) maple syrup

1 tbsp (15 ml) pure vanilla extract

1 tbsp (6 g) large flake nutritional yeast

½ tsp ground flaxseed

Dash of kosher salt

Extra maple or birch syrup, for serving

Vegan butter, for serving

Vegan powdered sugar, for serving

Preheat the oven to 400°F (204°C). Add all the sauce ingredients to a medium mixing bowl; toss to combine and evenly coat the strawberries. Arrange the mixture on a parchment-lined, rimmed baking sheet or casserole dish and roast for about 40 minutes, stirring halfway through. The berries should be soft and thoroughly cooked when done.

While the strawberries roast, slice the bread, if not already prepared, and set aside. Whisk all the remaining toast ingredients together in a small bowl or liquid measuring cup. Pour into a pie dish or large, rimmed plate and set aside.

When the strawberries are done, remove them from the oven and mash with a fork, mixing together the berries and their juices. Transfer to a small bowl.

Heat a large cast iron skillet over medium and coat with a nonstick cooking spray. Working in batches, dip the French toast slices in the milk mixture for about 30 seconds to 1 minute per side, or until the mixture has soaked all the way through. Take care not to soak the bread so long that it starts to disintegrate. Cook as many as you can fit in the pan for 3 to 5 minutes per side, until browned. Repeat with remaining slices.

Serve hot with a pad of butter, a dusting of powdered sugar and a slathering of the roasted strawberry sauce.

notes: Use a loaf of French bread for this toast. Larger than a baguette and similar to a loaf of Italian bread (used in making garlic bread) the French loaf is not as wide and a bit taller. Fresh bread can usually be purchased in the cake/bakery section of your local grocery store.

Any leftover strawberry sauce is heavenly stirred into vegan yogurt or served atop vegan ice cream.

tofu veggie scramble w/ roasted potatoes

This is Todd's *ultimate* breakfast. I'll often make the roasted potatoes the night before and then quickly fix the scrambled tofu in the morning. The use of a pressure cooker makes the scramble part a snap, but I've included conventional stove-top directions, as well.

Usually, we fashion this dish into a breezy breakfast burrito, however, sometimes we just eat it plain atop buttery toast. It's a comforting and hearty breakfast that will please omnivores and vegans alike.

serves 4

Potatoes

10 medium (1.5 kg) red and/or Yukon gold potatoes, scrubbed and diced

2 tbsp (30 ml) olive oil

1 tbsp (3 g) dried rosemary

½ tbsp (8 g) kosher salt

½ tsp onion powder

½ tsp garlic powder

¼ tsp ground black pepper

Scramble

½ tbsp (7 ml) olive oil

1 (250 g) medium yellow onion, diced small

2 large (10 g) garlic cloves, minced

¾ cup (180 ml) vegetable broth

3 (100 g) small carrots, diced small

3 (130 g) medium celery stalks, sliced

1 ½ cups (100 g) fresh kale leaves, destemmed and chopped small

12 oz (340 g) extra-firm tofu, drained and hand-crumbled into bite-size pieces

½ tsp ground turmeric

¼ tsp chili powder

½ tsp Kala Namak salt or kosher salt

¼ tsp paprika

¼ tsp ground black pepper

¼ cup (20 g) large-flake nutritional yeast

Preheat the oven to 400°F (204°C).

Dice the potatoes and place them in a large mixing bowl. Toss with the olive oil. Add the remaining potato ingredients to a small bowl and mix to combine. Now, add the spice mixture to the potatoes, tossing well to coat. Arrange evenly on a parchment lined or large baking sheet coated with nonstick cooking spray. Roast for 50 minutes, stirring halfway through, until golden brown and tender.

While the potatoes roast, heat the olive oil for the scramble in a pressure cooker or large soup pot over medium-low. Add the onion and garlic; sauté for about 5 minutes, until fragrant.

Deglaze the pan with the vegetable broth and add the remaining scramble ingredients. Stir well to combine. At this point, turn the heat to high and bring to high pressure. Cook at high pressure for 5 minutes, then use a quick release method by running cold water over the pot. Alternatively, bring the liquid to a boil, then cover and reduce to a simmer. Simmer for 15–20 minutes, or until the carrots are tender.

Remove from heat and stir in the nutritional yeast.

Serve the potatoes along with scramble. We like to eat this breakfast with homemade bread and a fruit salad.

pan-fried polenta cakelets w/ caramelized rhubarb rum sauce

In the birth of summer, we always have an abundance of rhubarb. There's rhubarb in the garden, rhubarb is fervently bestowed upon folks by friends and family, rhubarb is even *deliberately* abandoned in the breakroom at work with a "Please take me!!" Post-it note taped to the bag; begging for some compassionate soul to come scoop it up. *Surprise, surprise*—it's always *me*. Honestly though, why aren't people *jumping* at the chance for more rhubarb in their lives?! What I am trying to say is that I *always* have fresh rhubarb around. It's incredible married with polenta and fashions itself into a humble, but scrumptious breakfast. I like to slightly caramelize the rhubarb by roasting it with rum and brown sugar. Then, cooked polenta is poured over and allowed to set. Cut out fun shapes (or just squares) and fry up it up in a cast iron skillet, then drizzle with a sweet rhubarb rum sauce. The entire thing can be made the day before and stored in the fridge. When morning comes, simply cut out the polenta to pan fry!

Rhubarb

6 large (328 g) stalks of rhubarb, cut into 1 inch (2.5 cm) pieces on the diagonal

1 tbsp (15 ml) pure vanilla extract

¾ cup (180 ml) spiced rum (see note)

¾ cup (100 g) vegan brown sugar, lightly packed

Polenta

2 cups (326 g) medium-grind polenta, dry (not the instant kind)

4 cups (950 ml) water

4 cups (950 ml) nondairy milk

¼ cup (60 ml) maple syrup

½ tsp ground cinnamon

½ tsp table salt

1 tbsp (15 ml) unrefined or refined coconut oil, for frying

Vegan powdered sugar, for serving (optional)

Maple syrup, for serving (optional)

Vegan butter, for serving (optional)

Preheat the oven to 350°F (177°C). Arrange the sliced rhubarb in a single layer in a large 9 x 13-inch (23 x 33-cm) casserole dish coated with a nonstick cooking spray. Stir the vanilla and rum together in a liquid measuring cup and pour over the rhubarb; sprinkle the rhubarb with brown sugar. Roast for about 45 minutes, until fork tender. Remove from the oven and carefully, using a large spoon, ladle out as much of the liquid from the pan as possible into a small pitcher. This is the rum sauce that will be served over the polenta. If the rhubarb got tousled about while extracting the liquid, rearrange the pieces in an even layer.

While the rhubarb is roasting, whisk together all the polenta ingredients in a large, heavy-bottomed soup pot. Bring to a boil over medium-high heat, stirring occasionally. Once boiling, reduce the heat to medium-low; whisk frequently to ensure that the polenta doesn't clump or burn. When it starts to thicken and there are no clumps, swap the whisk for a wooden spoon and continue to stir frequently until very thick and it begins to pull away from the sides of the pot. The total time for the polenta should be about 40 to 50 minutes; it should be done around the same time as the rhubarb.

Quickly transfer the cooked polenta into the casserole dish, covering the rhubarb. Use the back of the wooden spoon to smooth it out. Place a piece of parchment paper over the polenta and press down gently to even out the surface and press it into the rhubarb. This will help to ensure even frying.

Allow to rest for about 20 minutes, then cover with plastic wrap and place in the refrigerator to set. I like to do this the night before. Once the polenta is set, cut it into squares or circles as large as you'd like (about 6). Heat the coconut oil in a large, cast iron skillet over medium. Fry the polenta for about 10 to 15 minutes per side, until golden brown.

Heat the rum sauce in the microwave for 30 seconds. Serve the fried polenta hot, with a drizzling of the sauce or maple syrup, a pad of butter and a bit of powdered sugar.

note: Not all of the alcohol will be evaporated during the cooking process (though much of it will). If you like, feel free to reduce the alcohol to about ¼ cup (60 ml) or simply omit altogether. Just sprinkle the brown sugar over the rhubarb to roast and when ready to serve, use maple syrup in place of the sauce.

scallion & garlic steamed buns w/ asian dipping sauce

I know what you're thinking: Why on earth is this recipe in the *breakfast* chapter? Well, have you had a delicious and warm, garlicky, freshly steamed bun (or roll, as Todd calls them) in the morning? Probably not. So you can't really tell me it's not one the most humble and divine little savory breakfasts out there. I can, and it *is*. It's time to break away from the monotony of predictable breakfast fare!

There's just something about steamed buns, besides the giggle-inducing name (if you happen to have third-grade humor like me). I like to serve these soft rolls with a side of my Spot-On Scrambled "Eggs" (page 24) for a kind of Asian fusion inspired breakfast. The tofu is so easy to whip up while the buns are steaming! However, feel free to make these buns anytime you like. I confess they don't *have* to be for breakfast.

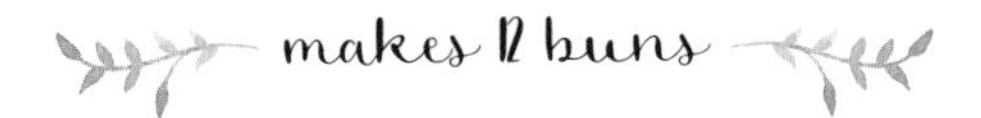

Buns

1 ¼ cups (295 ml) plain, unsweetened nondairy milk

½ tbsp (6 g) vegan granulated sugar

½ tsp active yeast

1 tbsp (15 ml) olive oil

3 cups (425 g) all-purpose flour

¼ cup (30 g) vegan stick butter

6 (25 g) large garlic cloves, minced

6 large green onion stalks, sliced on the diagonal

Sauce

¼ cup (60 ml) soy sauce

2 tbsp (30 ml) rice wine vinegar

1 tbsp (15 ml) agave nectar or maple syrup

½ tbsp (7 ml) sesame oil

Dash of red pepper flakes

In a microwave-safe measuring cup, microwave the milk for about 60–90 seconds (until hot but not too hot to hold a finger in it, about 110°F [43°C]). Pour the milk into a large electric mixing bowl. By hand, whisk the sugar into the milk, and then stir in the yeast with a wooden spoon. Allow the mixture to rest for about 5 to 10 minutes until a foamy blanket has formed.

Preheat the oven as low as it will go, usually about 200°F (93°C). Once it reaches temperature, turn it off and leave the door open for a few minutes before shutting. When the yeast is ready, pour the oil into the yeast mixture—no need to stir. Slowly add the flour into the liquid, using the wooden spoon to mix, until it forms a ragged dough mess. Fix the bowl to the electric mixing stand using the dough hook attachment. Knead on speed 2–4 for about 8 to 10 minutes until the dough is elastic and smooth and has pulled away from the sides of the bowl. The bowl should be clean of dough at this point with none sticking to the sides. Alternatively, the dough can be kneaded by hand on a floured surface.

Turn the dough out and form a ball. Coat the mixing bowl with a nonstick cooking spray and place the dough ball back into the bowl. Cover loosely with plastic wrap or a damp tea towel (not terry cloth) and allow to rest in the oven with the door shut for about 1 hour or until it's doubled in size. Once the dough has proofed, remove from the oven and cut into 12 equal pieces, forming them into balls; allow the balls to rest. In a small frying pan, heat the butter over medium-low. Add the garlic and sauté for about 3 to 5 minutes, until fragrant and slightly golden. Remove from heat. Place the green onions in a small bowl.

Roll each dough ball into a long oval shape, about 3 x 5 inches (7.6 x 13 cm). Slice 5 to 6 vertical slits in the middle of the oval, from the top to the bottom, leaving the top and bottom still intact. Using a pastry brush, brush on some of the garlic butter and top with a sprinkling of the scallions. Grasping the top and the bottom of the oval, twist the dough in opposite directions then swirl to make a bun shape, pressing to seal the ends together. Repeat with a few more of the dough balls—as many as you can fit in the steamer without touching.

Coat the inside of the steamer with a nonstick cooking spray or place the buns on a small square of parchment paper and steam for about 12 minutes, ensuring they aren't touching. Once the time is up, unplug the steamer or remove from heat and allow to rest for 3 minutes with the lid still closed. Open the lid slowly once done and remove the buns from the steamer. Repeat with remaining dough balls.

While the buns steam, make the sauce by whisking all the ingredients together in a small bowl. Serve the buns warm with the dipping sauce.

afternoons

simple dishes for an easy lunch or a speedy dinner

Afternoon fare holds my favor. It's often the first meal of the day for me if I'm feeling unusually peckish. I think the best thing about lunch is that it's essentially dinner, but made quick and simple. A respite in the middle of a busy day that demands pause. An often predetermined time to rest, reflect and chow down on some seriously delicious food. Who knows, maybe even get in some light reading?

These are fast and simple dishes that whip up easily for lunch or come to the rescue if you're in a bind for dinner. I feature lighter dishes that are hearty enough to satisfy after your morning's fuel has well been expended and still keep you content far into the evening, just in time for dinner.

Many of these afternoon meals are household staples, such as the "Tuna" Waldorf Salad Sandwiches (page 38), which makes at least a biweekly appearance. I needed a substitute to fill the void after growing up on Copper River salmon sandwiches my entire life and I've found this to be the best one yet. My Easy Vegan Ramen (page 49) makes for a quick and straightforward meal when you're craving something nostalgic and perhaps a bit naughty. For a super-healthy lunch try my Summer Veggie Quinoa & Rice Bowl (page 54); it's just what you're looking for. I make this bowl at least weekly, using whatever vegetables and grains I have on hand. It's exceptionally adaptable and with so many variations, it'll never get tiresome. Pastas, sandwiches, wraps and more are just a few of the delicious dishes you'll find in the following pages.

"tuna" waldorf salad sandwiches

As a native Alaskan, I grew up toting along a wild-salmon salad sandwich to school every day for lunch. Once in a blue moon, when I *did* have a real tuna salad sandwich, it was quite a treat! This might be the reason that I often crave tuna or salmon salad sandwiches. By using chickpeas I can satisfy my odd craving in a healthy and cruelty-free way. It's amazing how well mashed chickpeas step in as the perfect substitution!

Crisp apple, crunchy walnuts and dried cranberries star in this Waldorf variation. This salad is great for sandwiches or perfectly delectable on its own. It's a super easy and really delicious recipe that's a wonderful replacement for traditional tuna salad—even omnivores agree!

makes 6 sandwiches

2 (15.5-oz [878-g]) cans of chickpeas, drained and rinsed (see note)

½ cup (125 g) vegan mayonnaise

2 (90 g) stalks of celery (leaves included), chopped

1 small (200 g) apple, cored and diced small

½ small (200 g) red onion, minced

¼ cup (65 g) dried cranberries

¼ cup + 2 tbsp (60 g) walnuts, chopped

¼ cup (5 g) fresh parsley, chopped

1 tbsp (15 g) stone-ground, Dijon or yellow mustard (optional)

1 tbsp (15 g) sweet pickle relish or minced sweet pickles (optional)

¼ tsp table salt

¼ tsp ground black pepper

Dash of kelp granules or seasoning (optional, see note)

12 slices of your favorite sandwich bread

In a food processor, add the chickpeas and pulse several times until they become a somewhat "flaky" consistency. They should not be whole, but not completely mashed either.

In a large mixing bowl, combine the remaining ingredients and mix well. Then, stir in the flaked chickpeas to combine. If I'm in a real hurry and the salad is just for me, I'll add everything whole to the food processor to chop, then pulse in the chickpeas. However, it can result in large pieces of celery and apple, so I do suggest the first method if you have the time.

Serve chilled, between two slices of your favorite sandwich bread, in a lettuce cup or solo!

notes: Save the chickpea water to make some of the delicious desserts you'll find in this book such as my White Russian Tiramisu (page 87), Cappuccino Meringues (page 183) or Cardamom Spiced Nectarine Cupcakes w/ Fluffy Meringue (page 188)! It will keep in the fridge for about one week.

I like to add a little dash of kelp seasoning to lend a clean, ocean essence, but it's totally optional. Kelp granules can be found in Asian and Hawaiian markets (as it's often used atop rice), but it's also available online at Amazon.com.

pea & sausage pesto crepes w/ creamy cheese sauce

This crepe recipe, born from an unfortunate lack of veggies in the house, is comprised of crepes filled with a pesto, pea and sausage mixture that's laid atop baby greens and fresh tomatoes, drizzled with a creamy cheese sauce. It's now one of my most beloved crepe recipes. The sweet peas mingle deliciously with the rich pesto, savory sausage and bright tomato. The sauce ties it all together into an elegant dish fit for French royalty! Crepes, while traditionally wonderful for brunch or lunch, also make an absolutely terrific breakfast and even dinner.

makes 7 (12-inch [30-cm]) crepes

Batter

1 ⅔ cups (250 g) all-purpose flour

2 tbsp (15 g) cornstarch

2 tbsp (25 g) vegan granulated sugar

½ tsp Kala Namak salt or table salt

⅛ tsp ground turmeric

1 ½ cups (350 ml) plain, unsweetened soy milk

¾ cup (180 ml) canned chickpea water

2 tbsp (30 ml) olive oil

Filling

1 (12-oz [340-g]) package of frozen peas (or equal amount of fresh peas)

¼ cup (60 g) vegan pesto, homemade or store-bought (see note)

1 (95 g) Field Roast Italian Vegan Sausage or equivalent, chopped

1 tsp fresh thyme or ¼ tsp dried thyme

assorted baby greens

1 medium (140 g) tomato, diced small

Cheese Sauce

2 tbsp (30 g) vegan stick butter

1 ¼ cup (300 ml) plain, unsweetened soymilk

½ cup (120 ml) water

½ cup + 2 tbsp (50 g) large-flake nutritional yeast

2 tbsp (25 g) all-purpose flour

1 tbsp (15 ml) yellow mustard

1 tsp kosher salt

½ tsp garlic powder

½ tsp onion powder

Scant ½ tsp ground black pepper

In a large bowl, whisk together the ingredients from the flour through the turmeric. Whisk the soy milk, chickpea liquid and oil into the dry mixture until smooth. Cover and allow to rest at room temperature for about 30 minutes.

While the batter rests, make the filling by defrosting and warming the peas in a microwave-safe dish for about 2 minutes on defrost and then 1 to 2 minutes on high. Place the peas and pesto in a food processor and pulse until coarsely mashed and well combined. Pulse or stir in the chopped sausage and thyme. Set aside.

To make the cheese sauce, melt the butter in small saucepan over medium-low heat. Whisk in the remaining ingredients until it's smooth. Continue to heat for about 3 minutes, whisking occasionally; remove from heat and set aside.

Once the batter is done resting, heat a 12-inch (30-cm) large cast iron skillet coated with a nonstick cooking spray over medium-high. Test if it's hot enough by flicking a droplet of water into the pan; if it sizzles, then it's ready. Using a ½ cup (120 ml) measuring cup, ladle the batter onto the hot pan. Tilt the pan in a circle, allowing the batter to fill the entire base of the pan. Heat for about 3 minutes, until just slightly golden and the top is firm to the touch. Flip using a skinny, heat-proof spatula by sliding it around the edges to loosen the crepe, then down the middle of the crepe. Heat for 1 minute then transfer to a large plate and repeat with remaining batter or as many crepes as you'd like to make.

At this time, quickly reheat the filling mixture and the sauce if necessary. Fill half of a crepe with a small handful of fresh baby greens, then top with the pea mixture and tomato; add a drizzling of cheese sauce. Fold over the empty side of the crepe, making a half circle, then drizzle more sauce on top. Serve warm. Saved batter can be stored in the fridge and used within 4 days. Use any remaining cheese sauce as a dip, stirred into pasta or on sandwiches!

notes: Most pesto contains Parmesan cheese. I always make my own to ensure that it's vegan. In this book you'll find pesto recipes using chard (page 106), beet (page 78) and fennel frond (page 85)!

If you have a smaller cast iron pan, you'll need to adjust the amount of batter used. I strongly recommend using a cast iron pan or a large crepe pan as opposed to a regular frying pan; crepes can sometimes stick to a regular pan.

soba & veggie miso bowl

This is a quick and super nutritious soup that's very easy to whip up. Soba noodles mingle with sweet carrots, savory shiitake mushrooms, elegant broccolini and snap peas, all nestled in a hearty soy-miso broth.

I crave this clean-eating soup on cold and dreary days when I need a good, healthy meal to get me going. There are a lot of chilly days in Alaska, so I find myself making this meal often. It's also super adaptable, so feel free to substitute any veggies of your pleasing.

makes 3 large bowls

4 oz (112 g) soba noodles, dry

3 cups (700 ml) vegetable broth

3 cups (700 ml) water

1 medium (74 g) carrot, sliced on the diagonal

¼ cup (18 g) dried shiitake mushrooms (or ½ cup [37 g] fresh), chopped

5 cups (226 g) raw broccolini (baby broccoli), ends trimmed (see note)

1 cup (68 g) snap peas, halved diagonally

1 tbsp (30 g) red miso paste

2 tbsp (30 ml) soy sauce

Bring a small pot of water to boil for the noodles. Once boiling, add the noodles and cook for 4 minutes. Drain and rinse with cold water. Set aside.

While the water boils for the noodles, add the vegetable broth and water to a medium saucepan. Turn the heat to high and bring to a gentle boil. Add the carrots and chopped dried mushrooms.

Halve the broccolini so that the floret ends are bite size. The stems can either be left intact or sliced on the diagonal for easier consumption. Add the broccolini florets and stems to the saucepan with the broth and water. Allow them to cook for about 10 to 15 minutes, or until tender. When there are about 2 minutes left, add the peas.

Once the carrots, mushrooms and broccolini are all tender, remove the soup from heat. Dip out about ½ cup (120 ml) of the soup broth and whisk in the miso paste until smooth. Stir the miso broth back into the soup along with the soy sauce.

To serve, divide the cooked noodles evenly among three large bowls. Then, evenly distribute the broth and veggies on top of the noodles. Serve hot!

note: If broccolini isn't available, feel free to use regular broccoli or broccoli rabe.

herbed socca w/ roasted broccoli & hummus

I like to think of socca as "lazy man's pizza," but it's really better thought of as a savory and hearty pancake made with chickpea flour. Just like with pizza, any of your favorite veggies can be thrown on top! Even if it's just topped with a handful of mixed greens and some olive oil, it will be completely delicious.

Personally, I think socca batter is best when infused with herbs and/or spices and baked in a cast iron skillet. Okay—*truthfully*, it's best prepared in a wood-fired oven but we can't all live above an authentic, Italian pizzeria. A regular ol' oven works just fine, I assure you. My go-to socca is topped with creamy hummus, roasted broccoli and fresh sprouts for an easy and nutritious meal. Once you start making socca, it will be a regular in your arsenal of recurring meals!

serves 4-6

Batter

1 cup (90 g) chickpea flour (see note)

1 tsp table salt

½ tsp dried parsley

¼ tsp dried oregano

¼ tsp dried thyme

Dash of ground black pepper

1 ½ cups (350 ml) water

4 tbsp (60 ml) olive oil, divided

Toppings

1 small head of broccoli (200 g), sliced florets only

⅓ cup (90 g) of your favorite hummus

¼ cup (14 g) broccoli sprouts or microgreens (optional, see note)

Place a 12-inch (30-cm) cast iron skillet inside the oven and preheat to 450°F (232°C).

In a medium bowl, whisk together the batter ingredients excluding the water and oil. Now, slowly whisk in the water and 2 tablespoons (30 ml) of the oil. Allow the batter to rest for 15 minutes to 2 hours.

While the batter rests, slice the broccoli florets. Arrange the florets in a single layer on a baking sheet lined or coated with a nonstick cooking spray and drizzle with 1 tablespoon (15 ml) of oil. Set aside.

Once the batter is done resting, coat the hot skillet with 1 tablespoon (15 ml) of oil and pour in the batter. Place the skillet on the top middle rack in the oven and place the broccoli pan on the lower middle rack in the oven. Bake for 15 minutes.

Remove the broccoli from the oven after the time is up. Now, move the top rack to its highest level and broil the socca for about 5 minutes, until slightly crispy on top. Be sure to keep your eye on it, ensuring that it doesn't burn.

Remove the socca from the oven and allow to rest for 5 minutes. Top with a layer of hummus, followed by the broccoli and finally the sprouts. Serve warm.

notes: Chickpea flour goes by many names. You might find it labeled as garbanzo bean flour, besan or gram flour. It can be found in the ethnic or bulk section of your grocery store. Alternatively, it can be found on Amazon.com.

I grow my own broccoli sprouts so I always have them on hand. They're very easy to sprout, long-lasting and a lovely, fresh addition to meals, especially during the long, Alaskan winter months!

The longer the batter is allowed to rest, the better. But hey, when my tummy is growling, time is of the essence!

warm tempeh sandwich w/ wasabi sesame aioli

The first time I ever encountered tempeh was when I was a cook up at Hatcher Pass Lodge in Palmer, Alaska. We had a tempeh sandwich on the menu and I remember thinking what an odd thing it was, this fermented soybean cake. I had never seen it before! However, I soon fell in love with its subtle, unique taste.

Tempeh is nutty, chewy, absolutely wholesome and totally delicious. It doesn't have a very prominent flavor, so it's important to pair it with something zesty! I created a wasabi and sesame aioli that is the perfect addition to this Asian-influenced sandwich. I know you'll enjoy this warm and filling sandwich as much as I do.

makes 2 sandwiches

Tempeh

2 tbsp (30 ml) sesame oil, divided

8 oz (227 g) block of plain tempeh, sliced in half lengthwise

Aioli

½ cup (125 g) vegan mayonnaise

1 tbsp (15 ml) soy sauce

1 tbsp (15 ml) sesame oil

1 tbsp (15 ml) rice wine vinegar

1 tsp (4 g) vegan granulated sugar

1 tsp (9 g) wasabi paste

4 slices of your favorite sandwich bread (I use my Foolproof Sandwich Bread on page 149)

4–8 leaves of lettuce

In a large cast iron skillet or heavy-bottomed frying pan, heat 1 tablespoon (15 ml) of sesame oil over medium heat. Once hot (you can test this by adding one drop of water and if it sizzles, it's ready), add both halves of tempeh. Fry for about 5 minutes on one side. Then flip the halves, drizzle the other 1 tablespoon (15 ml) of sesame oil over top and fry an additional 5 minutes. It should have a crispy, golden-brown exterior.

While the tempeh fries, whisk all the aioli ingredients together in a small bowl. Toast the bread slices. Set aside the aioli and bread until ready to use.

To serve, slather each slice of bread with a generous amount of aioli. Add lettuce and one of the tempeh halves to each sandwich. Consume immediately.

notes: If not consuming straightaway, hold off on assembling the sandwiches as the aioli can make the bread soggy. If you have leftover aioli, it makes a great dip for vegetables or to drizzle over veggie burgers.

easy vegan ramen

Sometimes all I crave is a big, hot bowl of ramen noodles. You know what I'm talking 'bout. Before becoming vegan, the instant stove-top ramen used to work in a pinch. However, the seasoning packets have animal products in them and even the "Oriental" flavor contains milk proteins. Whaa? Drat!

So, I've created my *own* ramen noodles with a savory homemade broth. It's worlds better than store-bought, both for my taste buds and my health! It just takes a *teensy* bit longer to make than conventional stove-top ramen; definitely worth the extra few minutes. Nothing like a little desperation to change your life for the better! That *is* how Todd and I became vegan to begin with . . .

serves 2

Broth

0.5 oz (12 g) dried shiitake mushrooms (see note)

1 cup (240 ml) boiling water

½ tbsp (7 ml) sesame oil

½ tbsp (3 g) fresh ginger, minced

2 large (10 g) garlic cloves, minced

2 cups (475 ml) vegetable broth or vegan beef/chicken broth

1 (2 x 1 inch [5 x 2.5 cm]) piece of kombu (optional but recommended, see note)

½ (1.5 g) nori sheet (the seaweed for making sushi, see note), cut into small strips

1 tbsp (15 ml) soy sauce

¼ tsp fresh ground chili paste or red pepper flakes

2 medium (24 g) kale leaves, destemmed and chopped

3 oz (85 g) ramen noodles, dry (or 1 package of instant ramen noodles, packet discarded; see note)

8 (40 g) snap peas, halved diagonally

2 (9 g) green onions, sliced diagonally

In a small bowl, reconstitute the mushrooms in 1 cup (240 ml) of boiling water for at least 10 minutes, or until soft. Reserve the water.

While the mushrooms soak, heat the sesame oil in a large soup pot over medium-low. Add the ginger and garlic and sauté a couple minutes, until fragrant.

Add the remaining broth ingredients. Bring to a boil over high heat. After the mushrooms are done soaking, remove with a slotted spoon and once cooled, slice. Add the mushroom soaking water to the pot. Set the mushrooms aside.

Once the soup is boiling, add the ramen noodles, sugar snap peas and mushrooms. Boil for 2 to 3 minutes, then remove from heat and stir in the green onions.

At this point, I like to fish out the kombu, mince it and throw it back into the soup. However, it can be composted if you wish.

Serve hot.

notes: If using fresh shiitake mushrooms, use 4 ounces (113 g). Use 2 cups (475 ml) vegetable broth and 1 cup (240 ml) water; add the fresh mushrooms to the pot when the liquids are added.

This ramen is less of a soup and more like a soupy noodle bowl. If you prefer your ramen to be completely submerged in broth, try doubling the broth to 4 cups (950 ml).

Nori and kombu, both sea vegetables, might sound like exotic ingredients. However, nori is the seaweed used for making sushi and should be available at your local grocery store. I get my kombu online at Amazon.com. It's salty and oceany, and is great for soups. It helps your body digest those fibrous vegetables a bit easier.

Feel free to toss in some cubed tofu or tempeh, grated carrots, chopped bok choy, spinach or any other vegetables or add-ins you like.

mediterranean pita pockets

These hearty pita pockets are bursting with tart, crispy vegetables, salty Kalamata olives and a bit of creaminess provided by the hummus. This is a fantastic quick and healthy (and portable) lunch! My Mediterranean inspired pita pockets are a mouth-watering way to use up any extra tomatoes and/or cucumbers you may have lingering about in the fridge.

makes 3 pitas (6 halves)

Filling

1 ½ large (280 g) tomatoes, diced

½ large (121 g) cucumber, peeled and diced

⅓ cup (43 g) pitted Kalamata olives, chopped

½ small (50 g) red onion, chopped small

3 large (120 g) canned or jarred artichoke hearts, squeezed of excess liquid and chopped

¼ cup (4 g) fresh cilantro, chopped

2 tbsp (30 ml) extra-virgin olive oil

1 tbsp (15 ml) red wine vinegar

¼ tsp kosher salt

Dash of freshly ground black pepper

3 pita pockets, halved (see note)

3 tbsp (42 g) of your favorite hummus

½ cup (47 g) fresh romaine or leaf lettuce, chopped

Combine all the filling ingredients in medium mixing bowl. Stir well to combine and set aside.

Heat the pockets in the microwave for about 10 seconds to soften them; slice them in half. Next, spread 1 tablespoon (7 g) of hummus into each pita pocket (the two halves). Stuff each with ⅓ of the lettuce. Using a slotted spoon, place ⅓ of the filling into each pita.

Consume immediately.

note: If you can't find pita pockets, pita flatbread will work, too. Just use it like a taco! The juice from the filling can make the pita a bit soggy after a while, so make only as many as will be consumed immediately. These can be juicy, so get out the napkins!

creamy rosemary chickpea pasta

I've said it before and I'll say it again . . . chickpeas are the single most amazingly versatile, stereotypically vegan little balls of pure awesomeness out there. If there were a vegan MVP award for a food item, it would most definitely go to the incredible chickpea.

Here, I've used them to create a protein-rich, creamy sauce for this comforting shell pasta. Sometimes the best dishes are the simplest. Had a long day and need quick, healthy comfort food? This is fast food you can feel good about. Sauté up some garlic cloves, brown a few vegan sausages, infuse the chickpea sauce with fresh rosemary, parsley and nutritional yeast . . . voila! You have one tasty meal that's a perfect lunch or dinner and definitely kid-friendly!

serves 6

2 (15.5-oz [439-g]) cans of chickpeas, liquid saved from draining

1 lb (453 g) pasta shells, dry

2 tbsp (30 ml) olive oil

3 large (12 g) garlic cloves, minced

2 (190 g) Field Roast Smoked Apple Sage Vegan Sausages or equivalent, chopped (optional, see note)

1 tbsp (15 ml) soy sauce

¼ tsp ground black pepper

1 tbsp (2 g) fresh rosemary, chopped, or ¾ tsp dried rosemary

2 tbsp (14 g) large flake nutritional yeast

¼ cup (12 g) fresh parsley

Drain and rinse the chickpeas, reserving the liquid. Bring a large pot of salted water to boil for the pasta shells. Once boiling, add pasta and cook according to package for al dente pasta, about 10 minutes.

In a medium saucepan, heat the oil over medium-low. Add the garlic and sauté about 3 minutes, until fragrant. Add the sausage and fry until it becomes golden brown, about 5 minutes. Transfer the sausage and garlic to a bowl and set aside.

Add the chickpea liquid, about 1 ⅓ cups (315 ml), to the saucepan. If you don't have that much liquid, add water or vegetable broth to make up the difference. Add 2 cups (328 g) chickpeas to the saucepan and bring to a boil over high heat. Transfer to a blender.

Add the soy sauce, black pepper, rosemary and nutritional yeast to the blender or food processor. Blend on high for about 1 minute, until smooth. Return to the saucepan and add the remaining whole chickpeas. Smoosh them slightly with the back of a wooden spoon.

When the pasta is done cooking, drain but reserve ¼ cup (60 ml) of the cooking liquid. Set aside the liquid and return the pasta to the pot. Add the sauce to the pasta along with the parsley, garlic and sausage (if using). Stir to coat and allow to sit about 3 to 5 minutes while the pasta soaks up the sauce. At this time, if the pasta needs additional creaminess, add the reserved pasta water and stir well.

Serve hot.

note: The vegan sausage is optional, but I recommend it for some serious comfort food that's actually good for you! The Field Roast Sausage is the best around and it's found locally at many grocery stores and in certain Costcos as well.

summer veggie quinoa & rice bowl

Variations of this vegetable and grain bowl are one of my favorite staples in our home, *especially* during the summer months when farmer's-market zucchini, fresh garden herbs and sweet tomatoes are plentiful. It's a quick, easy and super adaptable recipe. I love to use whatever veggies come in my CSA box that week and any grain I'm hungry for.

This is a deliciously nutritious meal that could satisfy me every day of the week with all the variations I can think up. Please use whatever you have on hand! I hope this becomes a weekly staple in your home as it is in ours.

serves 4

Grains and Veggies

1 cup (190 g) quinoa/rice mixture, dry (see note)

1 ¾ cups (420 g) vegetable broth

½ tbsp (7 ml) olive oil

2 medium (538 g) zucchinis, quartered and sliced

1 small (228 g) bunch of baby broccoli or regular broccoli (see note), chopped

3 large (17 g) garlic cloves, minced

2 medium (24 g) green onions, sliced

2 cups (272 g) small heirloom or cherry tomatoes, quartered

½ cup (28 g) fresh parsley, chopped

¼ cup (11 g) fresh basil, chopped

Dressing

½ tbsp lemon zest

1 ½ tbsp (22 ml) fresh lemon juice

1 ½ tbsp (23 g) red miso paste

1 ½ tbsp (22 ml) agave nectar

¼ tsp ground black pepper

In a medium saucepan, bring the quinoa/rice and vegetable broth to a boil over high heat. Reduce to low and simmer, covered, for about 25 minutes until all the water is gone and the grains are tender. Or, cook according to package if using different grains. Remove from heat and keep covered until ready to use.

While the grains cook, heat the olive oil in a large cast iron skillet over medium. Add the zucchini, broccoli and garlic. Sauté about 10 to 15 minutes, until the veggies are tender; stir frequently.

While the veggies are sautéing, whisk the dressing ingredients together in a small bowl and set aside. In a large serving bowl add the green onions, tomatoes and fresh herbs. Stir well to combine.

When the veggies are done cooking, add them to the bowl and stir to combine. Add the cooked grains as well and pour in the dressing. Stir well to combine.

Serve warm or cold.

notes: Feel free to use all quinoa or all rice, if you wish. I like to use about equal portions of quinoa, red rice, wild rice and brown rice. Some Costcos sell 3-pound (1.36-kg) bags of the truRoots Organic Sprouted Rice and Quinoa Blend. It's great to have around! Alternatively, use any other grain like millet, farro or barley and cook according to the package.

If you can't find baby broccoli or broccolini, regular broccoli florets can be used. Feel free to use the stem as well, just be sure to slice them thinly enough so that they cook thoroughly.

healthier yakisoba

Traditional yakisoba is made with fried noodles, but I found myself wanting a healthier spin. Soba noodles turn out to be the perfect substitute! I keep this dish fairly traditional by making my own yakisoba sauce with the usual incorporation of Worcestershire and ketchup. Isn't it odd they're both vital ingredients to this well-known Japanese dish?

The soba noodles soak up this sauce beautifully; paired with tender, sautéed carrots and onions. This is a quick and zesty meal that's perfect for lunch, especially when you find your fridge deprived of produce!

serves 3

Veggies

½ tbsp (7.5 ml) sesame oil

2 medium (157 g) carrots (see note), grated or julienned

1 medium (242 g) yellow onion, half-mooned

Sauce

¼ cup (60 ml) vegan Worcestershire sauce (see note)

1 tbsp (15 ml) ketchup

½ tbsp (7 ml) rice wine vinegar

2 tsp (10 ml) vegan granulated sugar

2 tsp (10 ml) soy sauce

¼ tsp liquid smoke (optional)

⅛ tsp ground cinnamon

⅛ tsp ground cloves

⅛ tsp ground ginger

Dash of crushed red pepper

6 oz (180 g) soba noodles, dry

1 (10 g) green onion, sliced on the diagonal

In a large cast-iron skillet, heat the sesame oil over medium. Add the carrots and onion and bring the heat to medium-high. Sauté the veggies for a good 15 minutes, until tender and somewhat browned on the edges.

While the veggies cook, bring a large pot of water to boil for the noodles. Soba noodles need only a few minutes to cook, so wait to add them at the very end.

Whisk together the sauce ingredients and set aside.

When the veggies are done, remove from heat. Add the soba noodles to the boiling water. Cook for 3 minutes, then drain and add to the veggies along with the sauce and the green onion. Stir well to combine, using tongs to evenly mix the noodles, sauce and veggies.

Serve hot.

notes: If you have a mandoline to julienne the carrots on, it works like a dream.

You might think vegan Worcestershire sauce would be impossible to find because it normally contains anchovies. However, if you look to your store's "bargain-brand" version of Worcestershire, you'll see it's probably vegan by default. There are vegan specific ones, such as Annie's brand, or you can find a recipe online to make your own vegan version. Martha Stewart even has a recipe! The Worcestershire sauce is paramount to yakisoba, so don't skip it!

Feel free to add any additional vegetables you'd like such as cabbage, kale and so forth. If adding a great deal of additional vegetables (as I sometimes do), it's advisable to perhaps double the sauce.

lentil chickpea wraps w/ garam masala cashew cream

I love making wraps because they're so adaptable, healthy, quick and portable. What more could you ask for? I remember bringing these to our very first day of excavation on construction of our new home, so they hold a special place in my heart.

Garam masala is a savory, aromatic Indian spice blend that's composed of ground peppercorn, clove, cinnamon, nutmeg, cardamom, bay leaf and/or caraway. In this recipe it's the perfect complement to the warm lentils and chickpeas, and makes for a wonderfully complex, spiced cashew cream.

makes 6 wraps

Wraps

2 cups (475 ml) water

1 cup (178 g) brown lentils (see note)

1 (15.5-oz [439-g]) can of chickpeas, drained

Cashew Cream

2 ½ tsp (7 g) garam masala, divided

¾ cup (121 g) raw cashews (possibly soaked, see note)

¼ cup + 2 tbsp (90 ml) water

2 tbsp (30 ml) soy sauce

¼ tsp kosher salt

6 medium (294) flour tortillas

1 medium (142 g) vine-ripened tomato, diced

½ large (114 g) red bell pepper, julienned

2 cups (60 g) fresh spinach, washed and dried

In a large saucepan, combine the water and lentils. Bring to a boil over high heat, then simmer uncovered for about 15 to 20 minutes until tender. Drain and return to the pot. Add in the chickpeas and semi-mash the lentils and chickpeas with the back of a wooden spoon. Stir in ½ teaspoon of the garam masala.

While the lentils cook, prep the vegetables. To make the cashew cream, combine all the ingredients and 2 teaspoons (6 g) garam masala in a food processor and blend for about 4 minutes, stopping to scrape down the sides as necessary. It should be very smooth and creamy, with a texture similar to that of creamy peanut putter.

When the lentils are cooked, veggies are prepped and the cashew cream has been made, assemble all the ingredients at a workspace. Warm the tortillas by heating the stack of them in the microwave for about 1 minute, flipping the stack over halfway through.

To assemble the wraps, place a slathering of cashew cream in the center of the tortilla, followed by a scoop of the lentil and chickpea mash, then a few bits of tomato, strips of red pepper and fresh spinach. Tightly roll up the tortilla and slice in half. Repeat with remaining tortillas.

notes: Any lentil will work in this recipe, however, red lentils will end up being a bit mushy so I suggest avoiding those.

If you don't have a high-powered blender like a Vitamix or Blendtec, it might be necessary to soak the cashews for 2 hours in boiling water prior to using them. Just drain them when ready to use, discarding the water. This will help soften them, to render a silkier cashew cream.

sesame peanut soba noodles w/ sautéed mushrooms & snap peas

Everyone *must* have one really good peanut soba noodle recipe in their back pocket. My favorite is seasoned with sesame oil and topped with nutrient-rich sesame seeds. The earthy sesame flavor is the perfect complement to creamy peanut butter. Sautéed mushrooms and soy sauce offer a boost of umami while fresh snap peas cut through this dish with a bright crunch.

This Asian-inspired noodle dish is done in just about the time it takes to boil the water for the soba noodles. I always keep soba on hand for this fast and deeply satisfying meal. Feel free to add additional vegetables if you wish, such as carrots, bell pepper or whatever you like!

serves 4

Veggies

2 tbsp (30 ml) sesame oil, divided

4 ½ oz (125 g) cremini mushrooms, sliced

5 oz (140 g) snap peas, halved on the diagonal

Dressing

¼ cup (60 ml) soy sauce

¼ cup (72 g) creamy peanut butter

3 tbsp (45 ml) rice wine vinegar

3 tbsp (45 ml) agave nectar or maple syrup

1 tbsp (11 g) fresh ginger, peeled and sliced

1 large (5 g) garlic clove, whole

Juice from 1 lime, about 1 ½ tbsp (22 ml)

½ tsp ground fresh chili paste

9 oz (255 g) soba noodles, dry

1 tbsp (11 g) sesame seeds

1 medium (6 g) green onion, sliced on the diagonal

¼ cup (6 g) fresh cilantro, chopped

Bring a large pot of water to boil for the noodles.

While the water comes to a boil, heat 1 tablespoon (15 ml) of sesame oil in a large cast-iron skillet over medium. Pour the other 1 tablespoon (15 ml) into a blender. Add the mushrooms and peas to the skillet and sauté for about 5 minutes.

Add all the dressing ingredients into the blender; blend on high for about 1 minute until very smooth. Pour the dressing into the skillet and reduce the heat to low, stirring occasionally.

Once the water is boiling, add in the soba noodles. Cook for about 3 minutes or 1 minute less than the package calls for; they will be a bit undercooked. Drain them and add to the skillet, using kitchen tongs to toss the noodles and coat them in the sauce. Stir in the sesame seeds, green onion and cilantro.

Serve hot. This dish is best if consumed immediately or at least the same day.

notes: Any leftover noodles stored in the fridge can become a bit gummy. If you do have leftovers, stir in a bit of melted peanut butter and/or a dash of agave nectar or maple syrup before consuming.

vegetable chowder w/ arugula

What's more bone-warming and nurturing than a steaming bowl of chowder? Not a whole lot in my book! Unless it's chowder in a bread bowl . . . now *that* is the holy grail of comfort food and was always the first thing I ran to buy as a kid at the Alaska State Fair. We Alaskans eat a lot of chowder way up here in the north, though I confess it's usually of the seafood variety. I say, who needs seafood when you've got an abundance of Alaska-grown veggies? Let's leave the seafood in the sea and go for this chowder instead. Your heart and the creatures of the water will thank you!

This is a quick and easy vegetable chowder that's thick, creamy and oh-so-sumptuous. Chock-full of sweet carrots, crisp celery, tender potatoes, mouth-watering corn, creamy chickpeas and fresh arugula, this is one hearty soup that is sure to fill you up and warm your soul.

serves 4-6

1 tbsp (15 ml) olive oil

½ medium (156 g) yellow onion, diced

2 large (10 g) garlic cloves, minced

3 small (140 g) carrots, sliced

2 medium (102 g) celery stalks, chopped

2 medium (478 g) yellow potatoes, diced (see note)

1 (15.25-oz [432-g]) can of sweet corn, drained

1 (15.5-oz [439-g]) can of chickpeas, drained

4 cups (950 ml) vegetable broth

½ tbsp (7 ml) soy sauce

1 tsp dried thyme

½ tsp dried oregano

¼ tsp ground black pepper

¼ tsp paprika

1 tbsp (10 g) cornstarch

1 cup (240 ml) plain, unsweetened nondairy milk, chilled

2 cups (43 g) fresh arugula or spinach, hand-torn

Fresh parsley, for garnish (optional)

Heat the oil in a large, heavy-bottomed soup pot over medium-low. Add the onion and garlic; sauté for about 3 to 5 minutes until fragrant and the onions begin to turn translucent.

Stir in the carrots, celery, potatoes, sweet corn and chickpeas as you prepare them. Add the broth, soy sauce, thyme, oregano, pepper and paprika. Stir well to combine and bring to a boil over high heat. Reduce to a simmer and cover; cook for about 20 minutes until the carrots and potatoes are tender.

Once the soup is done simmering, whisk the cornstarch into the cold milk in a liquid measuring cup or small bowl, then slowly stir the cornstarch mixture into the soup. Stir in the arugula and heat the soup over medium for about 2 minutes or until the soup has thickened and the arugula is wilted; stir often.

Remove from heat and using a potato masher or the back of a wooden spoon, gently squash some of the vegetables in the pot to help further thicken the soup. You'll want it semi-chunky.

Serve hot with a sprinkling of fresh parsley.

note: Red potatoes, Yukon golds or other medium- to low-starch creamer potatoes will do well in this soup. Avoid high-starch potatoes like Russets, however, as they will crumble and fall apart.

evenings

both fuss-free and leisurely crafted meals

Ah, you're *finally* home. Time to relax and nurture yourself and those you love with a heart-warming meal that everyone will enjoy. Each person likes to enjoy their evening a little differently and the same is applicable to dinner. First of all, some of us call it *supper*, like my grandparents. There might be a technical difference between the two regarding the nomenclature, though I claim ignorance as to what it might be. They've always been interchangeable in my family. I playfully like to use *supper* when I'm feeling especially *Little House on the Prairie*; something I am ever more frequently being charged with. We can't yet decide on the name for this evening meal, so how can anyone be expected to come to an agreement on its characteristics and values?

Should dinner be quick and fuss-free or leisurely crafted with love? Should it simply be a delicious means to an end as a way to satiate appetites, or an elegant statement to our talents? Feeding a crowd or just flying solo tonight? Thankfully I have recipes for *all* of these circumstances. I confess, I don't always feel up to the task of making fresh pasta from scratch. However, it's so extraordinary that when I *am* channeling my inner Julia Child, I love making my Fresh Pumpkin Pasta w/ Creamy Pumpkin Alfredo (page 94). Sometimes I want a sure thing; something easy and reliable like my White Wine "Clam" Linguine (page 97). I usually prefer a lighter dinner like my Fresh Summer Rolls w/ Cilantro Mint Sauce (page 82), but that doesn't mean I don't absolutely crave the richness and comfort of my Baked Risotto w/ Mushrooms & Chard (page 86) from time to time. *However* you decide to have dinner tonight, there's a recipe in here just for you.

walnut-chickpea tacos w/ chipotle aioli

Tacos used to be one of those dishes I rarely made. I liked them well enough but even though they were quick to throw together, they always seem to be quite laborious. Not to mention how the proportions always seem to be off. This resulted in an excess of random ingredients I was never sure what to do with that ended up utterly forsaken, at the back of the fridge. *Nevermore!*

These tacos are truly outstanding and my absolute go-to taco recipe. I like to use cabbage and corn tortillas for a little Baja flair, as opposed to using leaf lettuce and flour tortillas. The walnut-chickpea taco meat is spot-on when you're craving those tacos you remember from your pre-vegan days. You'll forget all about them after trying this vegan variety!

Instead of using only walnuts for the taco meat, which I think would be too heavy and rich, I blend them with chickpeas to produce a lighter dish and create a contrasting texture as well as an added boost of protein. I know you'll enjoy these as much as we do!

serves 3-5 / makes 10 small tacos

Taco Meat

1 cup (156 g) canned or cooked chickpeas, drained (see note)

1 cup (123 g) whole raw walnuts

2 tbsp (30 ml) soy sauce

1 tbsp (5 g) ground cumin

2 tsp (6 g) chili powder

2 tsp (3 g) garlic powder

Aioli

¼ cup + 2 tbsp (85 g) vegan mayonnaise

2 tbsp (30 ml) fresh lime juice

½ tsp chipotle chili powder or cayenne pepper (see note)

Toppings

3 cups (155 g) green cabbage, shredded

10 (76 g) cherry tomatoes, halved

½ (202 g) avocado, chopped

½ cup (14 g) fresh cilantro, chopped

10 (235 g) small corn tortillas

Place all the taco meat ingredients into a food processor or high-powered blender. Pulse several times, until the mixture resembles taco meat. You don't want to process it into oblivion. There should be chunky bits of walnuts and chickpeas, and the spices should be well blended. Transfer to a microwave safe bowl and set aside.

Whisk together the aioli ingredients in a small bowl and set aside.

Prep the veggies. Microwave the taco meat for about 1 minute, until warm. Heat the tortillas one by one in a clean frying pan over medium-high heat for 30 seconds each or microwave the stack of them for about 15 to 30 seconds, to heat.

To assemble the tacos, place shredded cabbage on one taco, followed by taco meat and then the remaining toppings. Drizzle with a generous amount of the chipotle aioli, repeat with the remaining tortillas and serve.

notes: I know using only a portion of the canned chickpeas is obnoxious, but just throw the remainder in a smoothie or smoosh onto toast with a bit of avocado and nutritional yeast. Yum!

If you'd like the taco meat itself to be a bit spicy, feel free to add ½ teaspoon of chipotle chili powder or cayenne pepper to the mix, too.

Top with some vegan shredded cheddar cheese, if you're inclined!

miso split pea soup

My older brother's favorite soup is split pea, which inspired me to make a vegan version that he'd love to eat just as much as me. A big part of veganism is finding substitutions in recipes that result in a meal that's just as tasty as what you grew up on or as your old favorites. No need for a hambone in this soup. Let's leave the bones in the piggy, shall we?

This is a smoky and briny, complex split pea soup that's a vegan treasure! Miso paste and liquid smoke are added to lend that traditional salty and smoldering "ham" flavor. This creamy soup is prepared lightning quick in a pressure cooker, but I've included directions for a stove-top method as well.

serves 6-8

1 tbsp (15 ml) olive oil

1 medium (270 g) yellow onion, diced

2 large (10 g) garlic cloves, minced

1 tsp dried rosemary

1 tsp ground coriander

½ tsp dried oregano

½ tsp ground turmeric

1 tsp kosher salt, to taste

1 tsp ground black pepper

3 medium (400 g) boiling (waxy, fingerling, creamer) potatoes, diced

1 medium (80 g) carrot, sliced

8 cups (1.9 l) vegetable broth

2 ½ cups (450 g) dried split peas

3 tbsp (90 g) red miso paste

¼ cup (60 ml) hot water

2 tbsp (60 ml) apple cider vinegar

½ tsp liquid smoke (optional)

In a pressure cooker or heavy-bottomed soup pot, heat the olive oil over medium. Add the onion and sauté about 3 to 5 minutes, until translucent. Next, add the garlic and sauté a couple more minutes, until fragrant. Stir in the dried herbs, spices, salt and pepper.

Stir in the potatoes, carrot, broth and split peas. Increase the heat to high, cover and bring to high pressure. Keep at high pressure for 6–8 minutes, then allow a natural release. Alternatively, if using a heavy-bottomed soup pot simply simmer, uncovered, for 40 minutes. Then, cover and simmer for an additional 40 minutes or until the peas are tender. Stir occasionally to ensure that the soup doesn't stick to the bottom if using the stove-top method.

Remove from heat. Whisk the miso into the ¼ cup (60 ml) hot water and stir into the soup with the vinegar and liquid smoke. Serve hot.

forest bowl w/ blueberry balsamic vinaigrette

I love having homemade, wild-blueberry balsamic vinaigrette on hand for impromptu green salads and, so, occasionally find myself with leftover dressing. This dish came to me on one such day when I also happened to find our fridge apologetically bare; no greens to speak of except for a few stray stalks of kale leftover from the makings of a soup. A small gang of sweet potatoes had taken up residence on the counter and a bag of quinoa eyed me from the turntable. That's when the idea for this quick and easy meal popped into my mind! I knew this bowl would be a most excellent complement for my sweet and tart vinaigrette.

This is such a refreshing, beautiful and wholesome meal; nutritious vegan fare at its best.
Nuts, seeds and dried blueberries adorn steamed sweet potato, fluffy quinoa and tender kale that's all drizzled with a blueberry balsamic vinaigrette. Sounds like a forest feast to me!

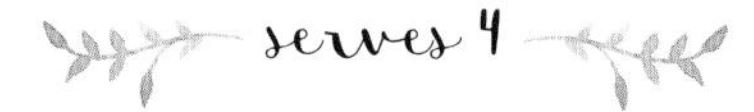

Bowl

1 cup (157 g) quinoa, dry

2 cups (473 ml) vegetable broth or water

3 small (564 g) sweet potatoes, diced

4 large (103 g) kale leaves, destemmed and chopped

¼ cup (46 g) dried blueberries

2 tbsp (14 g) chopped walnuts

2 tbsp (21 g) pepitas

Blueberry Balsamic Vinaigrette

½ cup (71 g) fresh or frozen and thawed wild blueberries

¼ cup (60 ml) quality balsamic vinegar

Juice from 1 small lemon, about 2 ½ tbsp (37 ml)

1 tbsp (15 ml) agave nectar or maple syrup

Pinch of kosher salt

Dash of ground black pepper

In a medium saucepan, bring the quinoa and vegetable broth (or water) to a boil over high heat. Reduce to a simmer and cover; cook for 15 to 20 minutes. Once done, the water should all be evaporated and the quinoa tender. Fluff with a fork and set aside.

Steam the diced sweet potatoes for 15 minutes, until fork tender, while the quinoa cooks. Add the chopped kale to a microwave safe bowl and microwave on high for about 1 minute until wilted. It should develop a bright green hue and still have a bit of chew to it. Be sure not to overcook it. Add the dried blueberries, walnuts and pepitas to a small bowl and toss to combine.

While the quinoa and sweet potato cook, make the dressing by combining all the ingredients in a blender; blend for about 30 seconds on high until smooth. Transfer to a small pitcher.

This dish can be served two ways: either combine the quinoa, sweet potatoes and kale into a large serving bowl and toss to combine, or separately divide them evenly into four bowls. Either way you chose, finish off each serving with a drizzle of the vinaigrette, to taste, and sprinkle with the dried blueberry, seed and nut mixture.

notes: Use what you have on hand for this recipe! Feel free to include your favorite greens, nuts, seeds and berries. Chard and spinach are great alternatives to the kale, dried cranberries or goji berries can be used in place of the dried blueberries and hazelnuts or cashews would be a good substitute for the walnuts.

If you don't feel like making the dressing, any fruity vinaigrette should be excellent.

foraged fiddlehead fern & roasted radish pizza w/ gruyere

Fiddlehead foraging is big in Alaska. Around mid to late May, you can find these new, tightly coiled fern heads sprouting cheerfully along streams and wet areas. Blink, though, and you'll miss their short season entirely. I've heard the little guys are available at farmer's markets and grocery stores in the States, though I confess I've never *seen* them for purchase myself. However, I should think one would most definitely prefer to adventurously forage them on the forest floor than picking them up in the store (if possible)!

This vegan pizza is sure to delight both your inner-hippie *and* your inner-foodie. It's sophisticated yet earthy, and will definitely bring your pizza game to a whole new level. Not fiddlehead season? Use asparagus or sliced broccoli stems!

makes 2 large pizzas

2 cups (121 g) fiddlehead ferns, cleaned

Pizza Dough

2 cups (474 ml) warm water (110°F [43°C])

2 tbsp (30 g) vegan granulated sugar

1 ½ tbsp (15 g) active yeast

5 cups (697 g) bread flour

2 tsp (12 g) kosher salt

¼ cup (60 ml) olive oil

Gruyere

1 ½ cups (350 ml) cold water

3 tbsp (45 ml) apple cider vinegar

3 tbsp (45 ml) tahini

3 tbsp (15 g) large-flake nutritional yeast

3 tbsp (20 g) quick-cooking oats

1 ½ tbsp (13 g) cornstarch

1 ½ tsp (2 g) onion powder

1 ½ tsp (2 g) garlic powder

½ tsp kosher salt

Toppings

5 large (96 g) radishes, washed and thinly sliced

¼ cup (6 g) fresh parsley, chopped

2 tsp (1 g) fresh oregano, chopped

Cornmeal, for spreading on pizza stone

Vegan butter, for running along crust (optional)

To begin, bring a large pot of water to boil for the fiddleheads. While the water comes to a boil, trim the stems to about 2 inches (5 cm) and give them a good rinse. Boil for about 3 minutes, until bright green; rinse under cold water. As you rinse, peel away any chaff (the brown leaves attached to the stems). Purchased fiddleheads might already be prepared. Set aside once cleaned.

To make the crust, measure out the water ensuring that it's the correct temperature. Add it to a medium mixing bowl and whisk in the sugar until it's dissolved. Next, sprinkle the yeast on top of the water and stir gently with a wooden spoon. Allow to rest for 5 to 10 minutes, until the yeast has formed a foamy blanket. Whisk together the flour and salt in a very large bowl.

Pour the foamy water slowly into the flour while stirring. Next, add in the olive oil and stir until it's well combined and looks like a shaggy mess. Then, sprinkle a liberal amount of flour onto a clean work surface and pour the dough out. Sprinkle more flour on top of the dough and knead by hand about 10 times until it's elastic and able to be cleaved in half. Form each half into a ball. Let rest at least 10 minutes.

While the dough is resting, place the pizza stone in the oven and preheat to 450°F (232°C). To make the gruyere, add all the ingredients to a food processor or blender; blend on high until smooth, about 2 minutes.

Transfer the sauce to a small saucepan and heat over medium-high, whisking frequently. The sauce will thicken and bubble, and should be done after 5 minutes. It should be the consistency of nacho cheese. Remove from heat and set aside.

Roll out one dough ball into a 14-inch (36-cm) circle. Fold over the edges of the crust to make a rim, pressing the seams together (optional). Once the oven is preheated, sprinkle an even layer of cornmeal onto the hot pizza stone and carefully transfer the dough to the stone. Bake for about 5 minutes, then run a pat of vegan butter, if using, along the rolled crust. Spread half of the gruyere onto the pizza then top with half of the blanched fiddleheads and sliced radishes. Bake again for about 13 minutes, until the crust is golden brown. Repeat for the second pizza.

Remove from the oven, sprinkle with parsley and oregano, slice and serve! Store leftovers in the fridge, wrapped in aluminum foil.

garden lasagna

If you grow kale and zucchini (or have it grown for you by your friendly local vegetable farmer) then you're pretty much set for this cruelty-free, delicious lasagna. Is vegan cheese hard to come by where you live or do you just plain have an aversion to it? *Never fear.*

This easy, veggie-packed lasagna is layered with a homemade cashew ricotta, and it doesn't need to rely on a processed, vegan mozzarella topping if you don't want it to. Feel free to whip up your favorite homemade tomato sauce or use a jarred one if you're in a pinch.

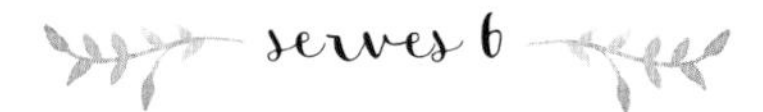

6 (138 g) lasagna noodles, dry

Veggies

½ tbsp (7 ml) olive oil

2 medium (431 g) zucchinis, diced

1 medium (141 g) green bell pepper, diced small

1 medium bunch—about 5 cups (140 g) fresh kale (I like Lacinato for this recipe), destemmed and chopped

Cashew Ricotta

1 ½ cups (202 g) raw cashews (see note)

½ cup (120 ml) water

¼ cup (22 g) large flake nutritional yeast

2 large (10 g) whole garlic cloves

¼ tsp kosher salt

24 oz (680 g) of homemade or jarred tomato pasta sauce (see note)

1 tsp onion powder

1 cup (66 g) vegan shredded mozzarella cheese (optional)

¼ cup (9 g) fresh basil, chiffonade

Bring a large pot of salted water to boil for the noodles. Cook lasagna noodles according to package for about 10 minutes or until al dente. Drain, rinse under cold water and cut in half horizontally so there are 12 halves. Set aside until ready to use.

While the noodles boil, heat the oil in a large cast iron skillet over medium. Sauté the zucchini and bell pepper for about 8 minutes, until somewhat tender, then transfer to a medium bowl. Add the kale to the skillet and sauté for about 5 minutes, until wilted and tender. Add the zucchini and bell pepper back to the skillet with the kale and stir in the pasta sauce (reserving ¼ cup [60 g] if not using vegan mozzarella) and the onion powder. Bring to a bubble over medium heat, stirring frequently, for about 5 minutes. Remove from heat and set aside.

To make the cashew ricotta, place all the ingredients in a food processor or blender and blend until completely smooth, stopping to scrape down the sides as needed.

Preheat the oven to 375°F (190°C). To assemble the lasagna, coat an 8 x 8-inch (20 x 20-cm) baking dish with a nonstick cooking spray. Spread a thin layer of the veggie mixture in the bottom of the pan. Next, arrange a single row of 3 (of the 12) noodles and spread ⅓ of the ricotta mixture evenly over the noodles. Cover with ⅓ of the veggie mixture, followed by 3 more noodles and so on, ending with the noodles. Top with the mozzarella cheese or pasta sauce.

Bake, uncovered, for about 40 minutes then remove from the oven and allow to rest for 10 minutes prior to cutting. Top with fresh basil and serve hot.

notes: If you don't have a high-powered blender like a Vitamix or Blendtec, it might be necessary to soak the cashews for 2 hours in boiling water prior to using them. Just drain them when ready to use, discarding the water. This will help soften them, to render a super-silky cashew cream.

Feel free to use your own, homemade tomato pasta sauce. You'll need about 3 cups (680 g).

unbelievable lo mein

This is one of my most beloved meals. It's easy to prepare and you will amaze your friends, family and even yourself with the most perfect vegetable lo mein. These wonderfully textured noodles are infused with a homemade, umami-rich Asian sauce and tangled with sautéed Napa cabbage, tender carrots and meaty shiitake mushrooms.

I developed this recipe after *inhaling* a mind-blowing lo mein from an Asian market in Anchorage after a long day of sofa shopping. I knew instantly that I had to recreate the comforting, warm bowl of noodles. Mine is just as tasty, though much less greasy, than its authentic counterpart. This is a revolving treasure in our house!

serves 6-8

1 oz (28 g) dried shiitake mushrooms, reconstituted (or 8 oz [226 g] fresh, sliced)

1 tbsp (15 ml) sesame oil

2 large (10 g) garlic cloves, minced

2 large (200 g) carrots, julienned

1 medium (925 g) Napa or Chinese cabbage, core removed and chopped

Sauce

¾ cup (180 ml) reconstituted mushroom water (or plain water if using fresh mushrooms)

½ cup (120 ml) soy sauce

3 tbsp (25 g) vegan granulated sugar

2 tbsp (30 ml) sesame oil

1–2 tbsp (15–20 ml) sweet chili sauce

Dash of crushed red pepper

2 (6 oz [340 g]) packages of tangled chow mein noodles, dry (not the fried variety, see note)

1 bunch (90 g) of green onions, sliced on the diagonal

Sesame seeds, for garnish

In a medium bowl, add the dried mushrooms and cover with a substantial amount of boiling water. Allow to rest until ready to use, at least 20 minutes. If using fresh mushrooms, simply slice and set aside.

In a very large rimmed frying pan or wok, heat the oil over medium-low. Add the garlic and sauté for about 2 minutes, until fragrant. Increase the heat to medium and add the carrots; sauté for about 3 to 5 minutes, stirring occasionally, while preparing the cabbage.

Add the cabbage and sauté until almost tender and wilted. This can be done in batches if the pan can't accommodate all the cabbage at once. Its volume will lessen considerably once wilted.

Meanwhile, bring a large pot of water to boil. While the water is coming to a boil, remove the mushrooms from their water with a slotted spoon. Slice and add to the veggies, stirring occasionally. Whisk together the sauce ingredients, including the ¾ cup (180 ml) of mushroom water, in a medium bowl or liquid measuring cup and set aside.

Add the noodles when the pasta water comes to a boil and cook for only 3 minutes. They need to be undercooked. Drain and add to the veggies along with the green onions. Stir well to combine.

Pour the sauce into the noodle/veggie mixture and continuously stir over medium-low heat for a few minutes until the liquid is almost completely gone. It will be ready when the noodles start to stick to the bottom of the pan a bit.

Remove from heat and serve hot, garnished with a sprinkling of sesame seeds.

note: It's important to use the right noodles. Use the nonfried chow mein noodles that are tangled, as opposed to straight. If you can't find chow mein noodles, you can use regular linguine. The noodles should still be undercooked. There will seem to be an excess of sauce, but never fear, the undercooked noodles will soak it all up!

tahini beet pesto pasta

Fresh basil and pine nuts don't always make an appearance at my local Alaskan grocery store. Oftentimes basil is just nowhere to be found and pine nuts are, of course, very expensive. Luckily, we always seem to have an abundance of beets! Especially during the cooler months, when basil definitely isn't showcased. What better way to make use of beets than blended in a creamy pesto?

Tahini, a somewhat bitter seed butter made from ground sesame seeds, marries deliciously with the sweetness of beets in this economical and nutritional powerhouse pasta. High in calcium and protein, tahini is a wonderful addition to any vegan or vegetarian diet. Beets cook at lightning speed when using a pressure cooker, but if you don't have one I've also included instructions for boiling them.

serves 6-8

1 lb (450 g) whole golden or red beets (about 4 medium, see note)

2 cups (475 ml) water

1 lb (450 g) dry pasta of choice (I like bow-tie or linguine for pesto)

Sauce

Heaping ¼ cup (60 g) tahini

¼ cup (40 g) large-flake nutritional yeast

Juice from ½ of a fresh lemon, about ¼ cup (60 ml)

2 large (10 g) garlic cloves

1 tbsp (23 g) red miso paste

1 tbsp (15 ml) soy sauce

1 tbsp (15 ml) sesame seeds (optional, as garnish)

Trim the beet greens so that 2 inches (5 cm) of the stem is left intact on the beetroot. I scrub my beets very well so I prefer not to peel them, but if you feel compelled to, you can.

Add the whole beets and water to a pressure cooker; cover and bring to high pressure. Cook at high pressure for about 20 minutes, then reduce the pressure by running the lid of the cooker under cool water. Alternatively, you can boil the beets. To do so, fill a large saucepan with water and bring to a boil. Add the beets, cover and cook for about 20 to 60 minutes, depending on the size of the beets; check them as you go. The beets will be done when they are fork-tender.

Meanwhile, bring a large saucepan of salted water to boil for the pasta. You'll want to wait to add the pasta until there's about 10 minutes left on the beets. Cook the pasta according to the package, about 10 minutes. Drain, but reserve about ½ cup (120 ml) of the cooking liquid. Return the pasta to the pot.

When the beets have about 5 minutes left to cook, add the sauce ingredients to a food processor and blend for 1 minute. When the beets are done, carefully trim the stem and tail off. Compost the scraps and roughly chop the cooked beets and add them to the processor; blend until very smooth.

Mix the pesto into the pasta and stir well to combine. Stir in as much of the reserved pasta water as needed to obtain the desired thickness. Serve hot and topped with sesame seeds as garnish.

notes: Be careful when working with red beets as they can stain. Golden beets are easier to work with in that regard and they are also less "beety" in flavor.

I like my pasta *exceptionally* saucy, so I add the entire amount of this pesto to the pasta. However, feel free to add as little or as much as you'd like and save the rest for use later!

general tso's seitan

This recipe was inspired by the General Tso's seitan at Whole Foods Market, although mine is baked as opposed to the traditional deep-fat-fried variety. I first tasted these little bites of heaven in Ohio and I *knew* I was going to have to recreate them. We currently have no Whole Foods up here in Alaska, so this recipe was born out of necessity!

There's no doubt in my mind that you'll love this dish as much as we do. It's an exceptionally tasty meal whose components time up perfectly. The dish is done and ready to inhale in about 30 minutes flat! Feel free to double the recipe if you have a crowd . . . or if you're just *real* hungry.

serves 2

Seitan

¼ cup (30 g) all-purpose flour

½ tbsp (7 g) ground ginger

Dash of ground black pepper

8 oz (226 g) cubed seitan (liquid reserved)

Rice

1 cup (183 g) jasmine rice, dry

1 cup (240 ml) cold water

Sauce

¼ cup (50 g) vegan granulated sugar

2 tbsp (30 ml) water

2 tbsp (30 ml) liquid from the seitan (or water)

2 tbsp (30 ml) soy sauce

2 tbsp (30 ml) rice wine vinegar or white vinegar

1 tbsp (15 ml) sesame oil

1 tsp cornstarch

1 tsp paprika

¼ tsp fresh chili paste

2 large (10 g) garlic cloves, minced

1 ¼ cups (119 g) sugar snap peas, halved diagonally

2 (18 g) green onions, sliced diagonally, divided

Sprinkling of sesame seeds, for garnish

Preheat the oven to 425°F (218°C). In a small bowl, whisk together the flour, ground ginger and pepper. Drain and squeeze the seitan, reserving the liquid. Roll each seitan cube in the flour mixture to coat completely, breaking apart any larger than bite-size pieces. Arrange the seitan on a baking sheet coated with a nonstick cooking spray. Bake for 20 minutes, flipping halfway through. Set aside when done.

While the seitan bakes, prepare the rice. Rinse the rice using a fine mesh strainer resting in a bowl full of cold water. Squish your fingers through the rice for a minute or two to remove the starch. The rice can be clumpy if the starch isn't washed away first. Combine the rice and cold water in the rice cooker. Do not stir, just push any rice bits below the water if they are stuck to the side of the pot. Cook until the rice cooker lets you know it's ready, then unplug and let rest at least 10 minutes, until ready to use. Do not open the lid. If you don't have a rice cooker, you can cook the rice on the stovetop according to the package.

While the seitan and rice are cooking, add the sugar and water to a small saucepan. Whisk a couple of times, then allow to come to a boil over medium-low heat, about 5 minutes. Stay close by to ensure it doesn't burn. Do not stir. Meanwhile, whisk together the remaining sauce ingredients in a small bowl, excluding the garlic. When you're sure all the cornstarch clumps are gone, whisk in the garlic.

Once the sugar water mixture turns a light amber color and begins to form bubbles all across the surface, whisk in the remaining sauce ingredients and simmer for just a couple of minutes, until thickened. Add in the peas and one green onion. Stir to combine and reduce the heat to low.

Once the seitan is done baking, stir the pieces into the sauce as well. To serve, divide the rice into two bowls and top with the seitan mixture. Garnish with the remaining green onion and the sesame seeds. Serve hot.

note: If using regular white rice or any other rice, you may need to adjust your water accordingly. However, I really prefer to use jasmine rice here. It's fragrant and perfect for Asian cooking. Plus, unlike basmati rice, it doesn't require soaking prior to cooking. Ain't nobody got time for that!

fresh summer rolls w/ cilantro mint sauce

Many people know these fresh, rice-paper-wrapped rolls as *spring* rolls, but in fact they are technically called *summer* rolls. Spring rolls are fried whereas summer rolls are fresh—who knew?!

This zesty green herb sauce was inspired by an upscale Asian-fusion restaurant in Anchorage, Alaska. As soon as I tasted the rolls paired with their green sauce, I knew I had to recreate the meal! This is a fresh, crisp and clean dish that's perfect for a warm and sunny day. If you've got a summer party, this recipe easily doubles for a crowd.

makes 4 rolls / serves 2

Sauce

1 cup (34 g) fresh cilantro, leaves and stems

½ cup (16 g) fresh mint leaves

¼ medium (65 g) yellow onion, chopped

2 tbsp (30 ml) water

1 tbsp (15 ml) fresh lime juice

1 tbsp (15 ml) agave nectar or maple syrup

½ tsp kosher salt

Dash of crushed red pepper flakes

Rolls

½ medium (116 g) cucumber, peeled and grated

2 small (60 g) carrots, grated

½ (75 g) avocado, sliced

1 oz (28 g) thin rice noodles (vermicelli), dry

4 (34 g) spring roll wrappers (see note)

½ cup (30 g) fresh mung bean sprouts (if they can't be found, see note)

4 large (5 g) fresh basil leaves, chiffonade

To make the sauce, add all the ingredients to a blender or food processor. Blend until almost smooth. If you have a tamper for your blender, use it to help encourage the herbs into the blade. Pour into a small serving bowl.

For the rolls, begin by boiling about 4 cups (950 ml) of water for the noodles. While the water boils, prep the cucumber, carrots and avocado. Once the water has reached a boil, remove from heat and submerge the rice noodles for about 3 to 5 minutes or according to package, until tender. Drain and set aside.

To make the rolls, begin by prepping your workspace. You'll want all the ingredients for the rolls within reach. Pour 1 to 2 cups (240–475 ml) of hot water into a very large plate or pie dish. Dip one spring roll wrapper in the water, completely submerging it. Allow it to soak for about 15 to 30 seconds, until pliable. Be careful not to let it soak too long or it will be become too soft and tear when rolled.

Carefully pick up the wrapper so as to not fold over any edges and lay it evenly on a clean surface. Next, add ¼ of the noodles, cucumber, carrot, avocado, sprouts and basil in the center of the wrapper in a horizontal strip. Roll up the bottom edge to the middle of the roll, follow by folding in the left and right sides, and then roll the entire thing away from you.

Repeat with remaining rolls and serve immediately with the green sauce.

notes: Be careful of adding anything that has a pointed edge (use shredded or grated carrots instead of julienned ones) because they can puncture the delicate rice wrapper and tear the roll. Feel free to play around with whatever veggies you'd like.

If you can't find mung bean sprouts, try sprouting your own mung beans or substitute with Napa cabbage or lettuce.

Be sure to buy spring roll wrappers, sometimes called "rice pancakes." They are large, circular, opaque white wrappers; *not* the refrigerated dough wrappers for wontons or egg rolls.

fennel frond pesto pasta w/ roasted zucchini & heirloom tomatoes

One of Todd's and my biggest misfortunes is that I absolutely *adore* everything pesto and he can't tolerate the stuff. I guess that means more for me? So I have to say it's pretty amazing, he actually really enjoyed this very mild fennel frond pesto.

In the summer, I love to make pesto out of chickweed. Yep, that weed you're constantly pulling from your garden makes one of the best pestos ever! It's decidedly earthy but in a good way. However, if you want a milder pesto, choose fennel fronds. These two pestos are some of the best I've ever had. I'm totally convinced that the more *scorned* a veggie scrap or weed might be . . . the better a pesto it will make! I've even made it with carrot tops, though they are quite strong in flavor.

Zucchini acquires a nutty, savory flavor when roasted and sweet; small heirloom tomatoes burst with tart juices. They both are an awesome complement to this creamy pesto that has just an intriguing hint of fennel. I love adding miso and soy sauce to add a little complexity and boost that umami flavor, which can be hard to come by when vegan.

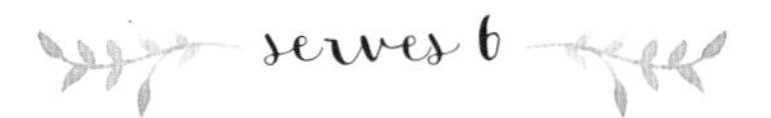

Veggies

2 medium (572 g) zucchinis, diced

1 pint (270 g) cherry or small heirloom tomatoes, halved

1 tbsp (15 ml) olive oil

Dash of kosher salt

17.6 oz (500 g) bow-tie, penne or other short pasta, dry

Pesto

2 cups (29 g) fennel fronds (see note)

¼ cup (60 ml) olive oil

¼ cup (33 g) pepitas (or sunflower seeds)

2 tbsp (20 g) walnuts

3 tbsp (14 g) large flake nutritional yeast

2 large (11 g) garlic cloves, peeled

½ tbsp (10 g) red miso paste

½ tbsp (7 ml) soy sauce

½ tbsp (7 ml) fresh lemon juice

Dash of ground black pepper

Preheat the oven to 450°F (232°C) and line a large baking sheet with parchment paper or silpat. Arrange the chopped zucchini and tomatoes on the baking sheet, drizzle with olive oil and sprinkle with salt. Roast for 25 to 30 minutes, until the zucchini is somewhat tender and golden and the cherry tomatoes are wrinkled. Remove from oven and set aside.

While the veggies roast, bring a large pot of salted water to boil for the noodles. Cook according to package, about 10 minutes or until al dente. Reserve ¼ cup (60 ml) of the pasta water and set aside. Drain the pasta and return it to the pot until ready to use.

To make the pesto, add all the pesto ingredients to a food processor and process until smooth, about 3 minutes.

Stir the pesto and the reserved pasta water into the cooked pasta. Serve, topped with the roasted zucchini and tomatoes on top. Alternatively, you could stir the veggies into the pasta but they might break apart a bit due to the stirring.

note: Fennel fronds are the hairy, carrot top looking frills on the ends of the stalks of the fennel bulb. Most people throw them away but they make an exceptional pesto! If you're not sure what to do with the bulb, it is delicious roasted! Slice the fennel bulb in wedges, arrange on a parchment paper lined baking sheet and drizzle with olive oil. Roast for about 40 minutes at 400°F (204°C) until fork-tender; use like any other roasted vegetable. The stalks themselves are quite woody and most people throw them out. However, I cut them up and add them to my veggie scrap bag in the freezer to make vegetable broth. No waste!

If you don't have fennel fronds, any leafy greens or herbs will do the trick, even broccoli, chickweed, carrot tops or kale!

baked sage risotto w/ mushrooms & chard

A few years ago, I would have shied away from making risotto, for perhaps a sort of odd reason. It's the everlasting *standing* involved. Is that your reason too? Risotto needs to be stirred almost constantly and I *literally* can't stand in one place for a very long time. Seriously! I actually had bilateral foot surgery to help alleviate the extreme and chronic plantar fasciitis that I've been struggling with since my teenage years. Thus, risotto just never found its place in my cooking repertoire. That is, until I discovered a *baked* risotto recipe in Sarah Copeland's cookbook, *Feast*. No more stirring? I'm on board!

I've adapted the recipe many times over the years, but my favorite way to have risotto is infused with fresh sage and topped with sautéed mushrooms and wilted chard. This is an easy recipe that's heavy on comfort, yet still maintains a healthy profile. If you want a *super-rich* risotto, throw caution to the wind and stir in a bit of vegan butter at the end!

serves 2

2 tbsp (30 ml) olive oil, divided
1 small (195 g) yellow onion, diced small
½ cup (103 g) Arborio rice, dry (see note)
½ cup (60 ml) white wine
4 ½ cups (1.1 L) vegetable broth, divided
¼ tsp ground black pepper
5 ¼ oz (147 g) cremini mushrooms, sliced
1 bunch (182 g) green chard, chopped (see note)
¼ cup (13 g) large-flake nutritional yeast
1 tsp fresh sage or ¼ tsp dried sage
Dash of kosher salt, to taste

Preheat the oven to 400°F (204°C). In a medium, oven-safe heavy-bottomed soup pot with a lid, or a dutch oven, heat 1 tablespoon (15 ml) olive oil over medium-low.

Add the onion and sauté for about 3 minutes, until tender and translucent. Stir in the rice, and then add the wine. Bring the heat to medium-high and cook, stirring occasionally, until the wine has evaporated from the pan, about 2 minutes.

Stir in 4 cups (946 ml) vegetable broth and black pepper; bring to a boil over high heat. Cover with a lid, remove from heat and transfer to the oven. Bake for about 55 minutes, until most of the water has been absorbed.

When there's about 20 minutes left for the rice to cook, heat 1 tablespoon (15 ml) olive oil in a large cast iron skillet over medium. Add the mushrooms and sauté for about 10 minutes until their water has evaporated and they are shrunken and dark in color. Transfer to a bowl and set aside until ready to use.

Wash the chard and chop off the stem ends to compost or use as a doggy snack. Add the chopped chard to the skillet and sauté over medium-low heat for about 10 minutes, until wilted. Remove from heat and add to the mushrooms.

When the rice is done cooking, stir in the remaining ½ cup (120 ml) vegetable broth as well as the nutritional yeast and sage; taste and add a dash of salt, if needed. Stir in the cooked mushrooms and chard. Serve hot.

notes: I really enjoy the silky texture of wilted chard in this recipe. Any chard will work whether it's red, green, swiss or rainbow. However, if you'd like to use kale in place of the chard, it will be great as well. Or, stir in spinach at the end to replace the chard.

A half cup (88 g) of dry pearled barley can be substituted for the rice; keep the liquid measurements the same.

This recipe can easily be doubled or tripled for a crowd.

sweet potato beet burgers

Veggie burgers are probably my biggest vice. They're easy to make, a great "fridge-cleaner," perfect for freezing, portable, fun and loved by all. I make so many different kinds, it's hard to keep track! My kitchen is pretty much always stocked with beets, sweet potatoes and chard thanks to my CSA box so this is my MVP burger.

I prefer to use ground oats as a binder, as opposed to rice or breadcrumbs, which elevates the nutrition profile, plus you don't have to cook anything! These cruelty-free burgers may look like they have a lot of ingredients but I assure you they are absolutely sans-fuss, and they're packed with protein, antioxidants and omega-3 fatty acids. I always have some veggie burgers stocked in my freezer. This way I can have a burger to zap in the microwave if I'm in a pinch. They really come in handy when you're on the run, don't have the energy to cook or find your fridge empty! Plus, they are oh-so-scrumptious.

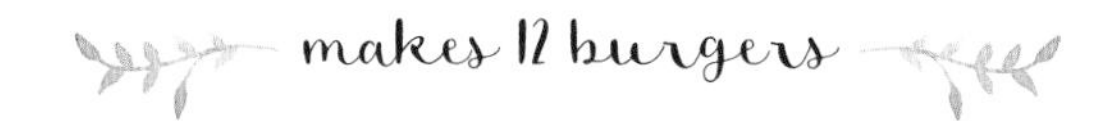

Burgers

3 tbsp (17g) ground flaxseed

¼ cup (60 ml) cold water

1 medium (424 g) sweet potato, unpeeled and cut into about ½ inch (1 cm) wide disks

2 tbsp (30 ml) olive oil, divided

¼ medium (165 g) yellow onion, diced

4 large (20 g) garlic cloves, minced

4 large (52 g) chard leaves (see note), destemmed and chopped

1 medium (178 g) uncooked beet, unpeeled and shredded

1 (15.5-oz [439-g]) can of chickpeas, drained

2 cups (184 g) old-fashioned oats, dry

½ cup (56 g) raw walnuts

¼ cup (60 ml) soy sauce

2 tbsp (30 ml) molasses

1 tbsp (16 g) tomato paste

1 tsp paprika

1 tsp dried basil

½ tsp ground cumin

Dash of ground black pepper

Toppings

12 hamburger buns

BBQ sauce or ketchup

Lettuce

Sprouts (optional)

In a small bowl, whisk together the flaxseed and water. Allow to rest for 10 minutes, or until ready to use.

Steam the sliced sweet potato for about 20 minutes or until fork-tender.

While the sweet potatoes steam, heat 1 tablespoon (15 ml) olive oil in a large cast iron skillet over medium. Sauté the onions and garlic for about 3 minutes, until the onions begin to turn translucent. Add the chopped chard and sauté an additional 5 minutes, until wilted. Remove from heat and set aside.

Cut off the stem and root of the beet and chop it into rough pieces. Feed it through a food processor with the shredding disc attached. Alternatively, it can be left whole and shredded using a box grater.

Add the chickpeas, oats and walnuts to the food processor and pulse to combine, scraping down the sides as needed. It should resemble a ground meat texture, about 10 pulses or so should do it; just enough so that the walnuts aren't left too large. Transfer to a large mixing bowl.

Now, add the steamed sweet potatoes and chard mixture to the food processor. Pulse to mash the sweet potatoes and transfer to the chickpea mixture. Stir well to combine.

In a small mixing bowl, whisk together the remaining burger ingredients and pour over the burger mixture along with the flaxseed. Stir well to combine and allow to rest for about 10 minutes.

Heat the remaining 1 tablespoon (15 ml) of oil in the same large cast iron skillet over medium-high. Form the mixture into roughly 12 burger patties and place as many as can fit in your pan at one time (I can get 4). Cook for 3 to 5 minutes per side, until a crispy brown crust has formed. Repeat with the remaining burger mixture.

Serve on a hamburger bun or wrapped in lettuce, with any toppings you like!

notes: Spinach or kale will work wonderfully in place of chard.

If you like, you can refrigerate the burger mixture for a few days and cook as needed. Or, cook them all at once and then freeze some, like I do.

red lentil soup w/ quinoa, lemon & mint

This is a slightly spicy and refreshing, yet hearty soup that is perfect for spring and summer. Loaded with complete proteins and exceptional nutrition thanks to red lentils and red quinoa, this soup gets its *zing* from mint and freshly squeezed lemon. I love to grow mint in my little garden, but be sure to grow it in a pot or else it can take over! If you have more than you can use, it can be easily dried and stored.

In a hurry? Should you require dinner in less than 30 minutes, I've included directions for a pressure cooker option as well as stovetop. There's nothing I love more than a super nutrient-dense, hot bowl of soup that can be done in flash!

serves 4

Soup

1 tbsp (15 ml) olive oil

1 small (145 g) yellow onion, diced

1 large (5 g) garlic clove, minced

4 small (118 g) carrots, sliced

2 tbsp (39 g) tomato paste

1 tsp paprika

½ tsp ground cumin

¼ tsp chipotle chili powder or cayenne pepper, to taste

4 cups (950 ml) vegetable broth

2 cups (475 ml) water

1 cup (172 g) red lentils (see note)

½ cup (100 g) red quinoa (see note)

1 tbsp (15 ml) soy sauce

1 ½ tsp (1 g) dried mint

½ tsp kosher salt

Dash of ground black pepper

Topping

¼ cup (32 g) sunflower seeds, toasted (optional)

1 medium (64 g) lemon, quartered

In a pressure cooker or heavy bottomed soup pan, heat the olive oil over medium-low. Add the onion and garlic; sauté for about 3 to 5 minutes until the onion is fragrant and begins to turn translucent. Stir in the carrots, tomato paste, paprika, cumin and chipotle chili powder; sauté about 2 minutes.

Add a splash of the vegetable broth to deglaze the pan, then add in the remaining soup ingredients. Stir well to combine; increase the heat to high and bring to a boil. Reduce to a simmer and cover; cook for about 20 minutes until the carrots are tender. If using a pressure cooker, increase the heat to high and bring to high pressure. Reduce the heat to stabilize the high pressure as needed and cook for about 7 minutes. Release the pressure by running cool water over the lid.

While the soup cooks, toast the sunflower seeds (if using) in a small pan over medium heat for about 3 to 5 minutes until slightly golden brown and fragrant. Be sure to keep an eye on them as they go from perfect to burnt *rather quickly*. Transfer to a small bowl and set aside.

Transfer half of the cooked soup to a blender and blend on high for 2 minutes, until smooth, with the lid vented so steam can escape. Stir the smooth soup back into the remaining soup.

Divide the hot soup into 4 medium soup bowls and garnish each with 1 tablespoon (8 g) sunflower seeds (if using) and squeeze in one lemon wedge. I like to pull the pulp off the lemon and plop it in as well. Don't skip the lemon, it's vital!

notes: I don't recommend using any other type of lentil in this soup recipe. Red lentils are split and thus, they cook much faster than traditional lentils. They're what give this soup its thick base.

Red quinoa is much firmer than other varieties of quinoa, which I find pleasant and toothsome in this soup. However, feel free to use regular quinoa, though it won't hold its shape as well. I get my red quinoa and red lentils from the bulk bin of our local grocery store.

flaky coconut tofu w/ creamy chard jasmine rice

This dish was inspired by a similar one we had at the cutest little vegan cafe in Hawaii. Todd absolutely loved the flaky, fish-like texture of the tofu and I knew when we got home I'd have to recreate it for him. This is one of Todd's very favorite meals!

Shredded coconut pressed into the firm tofu is what gives it that flaky texture. It's pan fried and laid atop a bed of jasmine rice stirred into a creamy, coconut-chard sauce. This is an impressive meal that even tofu haters will love.

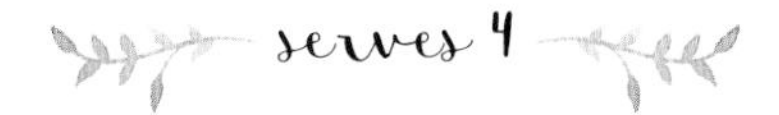

1 ½ tbsp (22 ml) unrefined coconut oil, divided

¼ medium (131 g) yellow onion, sliced

3 large (10 g) garlic cloves, minced

1 cup (240 ml) water

1 cup (186 g) jasmine rice, dry

14 oz (397 g) firm tofu, drained

½ cup (52 g) unsweetened shredded coconut

¼ cup (40 g) all-purpose flour

½ tsp kosher salt

¼ ground black pepper

1 medium (340 g) bunch of swiss chard or spinach, destemmed and chopped

½ cup (120 ml) full-fat canned coconut milk

1 tbsp (19 g) red miso paste

1 tbsp (15 ml) soy sauce

1 tbsp (15 ml) rice wine vinegar or regular white vinegar

1 tsp fresh ginger, minced

Dash of crushed red pepper flakes

Heat ½ tablespoon (7 ml) of the coconut oil in a large cast iron skillet over medium-low. Add the onion and garlic; sauté about 5 to 8 minutes until fragrant and the onions begin to brown slightly. Transfer to a plate and set aside.

Place the water in the rice cooker and rinse the rice thoroughly with tap water. Add the rice to the cooker and push down any pieces that are above the water. Do not stir. Close the lid and allow the rice to cook. When the cooker signals the rice is done (roughly 20 minutes), simply unplug the cooker and leave the lid closed until ready to use.

While the rice cooks, heat the remaining 1 tablespoon (15 ml) of coconut oil in the same large skillet over medium. Slice the drained tofu into 8 rectangles. Place the shredded coconut in a small shallow bowl and the flour in a separate small shallow bowl. Whisk the salt and pepper into the flour.

Dredge one rectangle of tofu in the flour, then press into the shredded coconut so it covers the entire piece of tofu. I even like to press some coconut into the center of the tofu so it bulges a bit. Repeat with remaining tofu pieces, then arrange them evenly in the cast iron skillet and fry over medium-high heat for about 10 to 15 minutes until browned. Flip and cook an additional 10 to 15 minutes on the other side. Remove from heat.

While the tofu cooks, place the chopped the chard in a microwave safe bowl covered with plastic wrap. Steam in the microwave for about 1 ½ to 2 minutes, until wilted.

Add the coconut milk to a blender along with half of the chard, including the liquid that is at the bottom of the bowl. Add in the miso, soy sauce, vinegar, ginger and red pepper flakes. Blend on high until smooth and creamy. Stir the coconut chard sauce, sautéed onions and garlic, and the remaining chard into the cooked rice.

To serve, divide the rice among four plates and top each plate with two pieces of the fried tofu. Serve hot.

fresh pumpkin pasta w/ creamy pumpkin alfredo

All you need to make easy, fresh homemade pasta is a rolling pin and a bit of elbow grease. No fancy kitchen gadgets here! There isn't anything in this world like fresh pasta paired with creamy alfredo sauce. You definitely don't want to skip this recipe!

I use canned pumpkin here; that way I can make this year-round! However, feel free to substitute the same amount of freshly roasted pumpkin purée if you can. Pumpkin and sage make a winning combination to form this divinely tender pasta dough. Creamy coconut milk lends itself for an incredibly dreamy alfredo that is sure to be a hit among your omnivorous friends and family. Salad? Forget it. Show them this is how vegans eat!

serves 4 / makes 1 lb 6 oz (630 g) pasta and 2 cups (504 g) alfredo

Pasta dough

1 cup (163 g) semolina flour

1 cup (137 g) all-purpose flour

½ tsp salt

½ tsp dried sage

1 (15-oz [425-ml]) can of pumpkin, divided between dough and sauce

4–6 tbsp (60–90 ml) water

Sauce

1 cup (240 ml) canned full-fat coconut milk

½ tbsp (7 ml) soy sauce

½ tsp salt

½ tsp freshly ground nutmeg

¼ tsp dried sage

¼ tsp ground black pepper

2 tbsp (8 g) large-flake nutritional yeast

¼ cup (4 g) fresh parsley, chopped

To make the pasta dough, add both the flours, salt and sage in a food processor fitted with the dough blade attachment. This can also be done in a large mixing bowl, if you don't have a food processor. Pulse to mix the dry ingredients, then add in ½ cup (123 g) of the canned pumpkin to the processor while it's running. Next, add the water 1 tablespoon (15 ml) at a time, while the processor is running. Process until the dough begins to form a ball at one side of the bowl; stop to scrape down the sides as needed. It should be fairly dry. Pick up a piece and squish it between your fingers; it should hold together nicely. If it's too wet, add flour 1 tablespoon (10 g) at a time. If it's too dry, add 1 tablespoon (15 ml) of additional water at a time.

Turn the dough out onto a lightly floured surface and knead by hand for about 5 minutes. Pasta dough is very firm and takes some muscle to knead. The dough should be smooth and not crack; it should have the feel of play dough. Roll it into a log and wrap in a tea towel or plastic wrap. Allow to rest for 20 minutes.

While the dough is resting, bring a large pot of salted water to boil for the pasta. To make the sauce, combine all the ingredients in a small saucepan over medium-low heat, excluding the nutritional yeast. Whisk in the remaining 1 ¼ cup (310 g) canned pumpkin until smooth. Heat over low, ensuring the sauce never boils; whisk occasionally.

Once the pasta has rested, separate it into four pieces. Roll one piece into a large rectangle on a lightly floured surface. It should be as thin as you can reasonably get it. Now, starting with the short end of the rectangle, gently fold the sheet up at 3 inch (7.6 cm) intervals to create a rectangular roll. Using a bench knife or chef's knife, slice vertically into strips for fettuccine. Toss the fettuccine with a bit of flour and set aside. Repeat with remaining dough balls.

When the water is boiling and the noodles are sliced, remove the sauce from heat and stir in the nutritional yeast. Add all the pasta to the water and boil for about 1 to 5 minutes. It really depends on how thick the noodles are, but they don't need long. The noodles should be firm, but not overly chewy and not mushy. Be careful not to cook the pasta too long, that's when it can become mushy. Continually stir the pasta to keep it from sticking together. Drain and return pot. Stir in half the alfredo sauce (store the other half in the fridge and use within one week or freeze). Top with fresh parsley and serve hot.

white wine "clam" linguine

Everyone has *their* signature dish. Well, this is my dish, as odd as it might be. It's the meal I most fondly remember preparing with my family and fittingly, the first recipe I ever memorized by heart. It's the very first dish I ever made my then not-yet husband, Todd, who marveled at how I threw it together sans recipe in less than 30 minutes. It might also be, dare I say, the only dish Todd and I have ever had an inside joke about. When I asked him one day early in our relationship what he wanted for dinner, he innocently didn't pronounce the "ee" sound at end of *linguine* so what came out was a shrill and overly-excited, "Clam lin-gween!" From then on, of course, we had to call it clam linguine . . . with a silent "e" at the end. *Clam lingween.*

I waited over two years since becoming vegan to make "clam" linguine, even though it's Todd's and my most beloved dish. I wanted to remaster and veganize that nostalgic recipe torn from the pages of a 1990s *Cooking Light* magazine for *a very long time,* but I dreaded and avoided doing so. It didn't even seem that *hard* to adapt. No, the real reason I waited so long was because I didn't want it to be different than I had remembered. I didn't want to lose those all those childhood memories tethered to the dish. Unfortunately, a big part of clam linguine (I know you're shocked here) happens to be clams and the juice they're canned in!

To this day I have never been more tickled with myself than being able to perfectly replicate the clam linguine from my cherished memories. Oyster mushrooms make an *unbelievable* substitute for actual baby clams, while vegetable broth with a bit of help from kelp crafts an oceany appeal that mimics clam juice wonderfully. This is a fantastic dish to share with your friends and family to demonstrate that vegan food is *just* as comforting and satisfying as its animal-based counterparts.

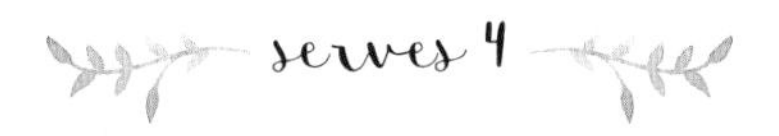

8 oz (227 g) linguine, dry

2 tbsp (35 g) vegan stick butter

1 tbsp (15 ml) olive oil

4 large (18 g) garlic cloves, minced

2 tbsp (15 g) all-purpose flour

1 cup (240 ml) vegetable broth

½ cup (120 ml) dry white wine

6.4 oz (182 g) oyster mushrooms, chopped into small bite-size pieces (see note)

¼ –½ tsp kosher salt, to taste

¼ tsp kelp granules (optional, see note)

Dash of ground black pepper

¼ cup (11 g) fresh parsley, chopped

2 tsp (2 g) fresh thyme, chopped or ½ tsp dried thyme

Bring a large pot of salted water to boil for the noodles. Cook according to package, about 9 minutes or until al dente, then drain and return to pot. The noodles will be soaking up some of the sauce, so be sure to slightly undercook them.

Melt the butter and olive oil in a small saucepan over medium-low heat. Add the garlic and sauté about 3 minutes, until fragrant. Whisk in the flour to make a roux, and cook for about 3 minutes, stirring frequently. Now, whisk in the vegetable broth and wine. Turn the heat to medium-high and add the mushrooms. Cook for about 5 minutes, stirring occasionally. Add in the remaining ingredients and cook for an additional minute.

Remove from heat and pour the mixture over the cooked noodles. Stir well to combine. It might seem like a lot of sauce, but allow the pasta to rest for about 4 minutes and the noodles will soak the sauce up to perfection.

Serve hot and with a lot of love.

notes: Oyster mushrooms can sometimes be hard to find. Should they elude you, feel free to use cremini mushrooms.

I like to add a little dash of kelp seasoning to lend a clean, ocean essence. Kelp granules can be found in Asian or Hawaiian markets (as it's often used as a seasoning atop rice), but it's also available online at Amazon.com or even at your grocery store in the bulk section. It can be omitted, but the linguine won't be quite as "clammy" tasting.

chickpea thai curry

To me, curry is one of those essential dishes like "tuna" salad, a bowl of roasted veggies and homemade bread. All are a vital part of my diet and put into *heavy* rotation in my kitchen. Thai curry can sometimes include a couple of unusual ingredients like fresh kaffir lime leaves and red Thai chilies, both of which just aren't accessible in rural Alaska. Never fear though, a squeeze of fresh lime juice and a dash of crushed red pepper flakes make exceptional stand-ins in this heart-warming curry.

The best part about curry, besides the way it tastes, is the way it fills the entire home with the most mouth-watering smells of sautéed onion and garlic, fresh ginger and fragrant curry paste. If you've never made curry, it's really quite easy and an absolutely divine, nutritious meal.

serves 4

1 cup (202 g) jasmine rice, dry

1 cup (240 ml) water

1 tbsp (13 g) unrefined coconut oil

¼ medium (91 g) yellow onion, diced

3 large (15 g) garlic cloves, minced

1–2 tbsp (15–30 g) Thai curry paste (see note)

1 tbsp (8g) fresh ginger, minced

5 small (136 g) carrots, sliced

1 medium (254 g) red bell pepper, julienned

1 (15.5-oz [439-g]) can of chickpeas, drained

1 (13.6-oz [403-g]) can of full-fat coconut milk

Dash of crushed red pepper flakes, to taste

2 tbsp (30 ml) soy sauce

1 tbsp (8 g) vegan brown sugar

1 tbsp (15 ml) rice wine vinegar or white vinegar

½ tbsp (7 ml) fresh lime juice

¼ cup (10 g) fresh cilantro, chopped

Rinse the rice in a fine mesh strainer with cool water to remove the starch. Drain and place in a rice cooker along with the 1 cup (240 ml) water. Close the lid and cook until the cooker alerts you that the rice is ready, about 20 minutes. Do not open the lid when it is done; simply unplug the cooker and allow the rice to rest at least 10 minutes or until ready to use. If using a stove-top method, cook the rice according to the package.

While the rice cooks, heat the coconut oil in a large cast iron skillet or heavy-bottomed soup pan over medium-low. Add the onion and garlic; sauté about 4 minutes, until fragrant. Stir in the curry paste and ginger, then add the carrots and bell pepper. Sauté about 5 minutes, then add the remaining ingredients excluding the lime juice and cilantro. Stir well to combine and increase the heat to medium. Allow to bubble gently for about 8 to 10 minutes, stirring occasionally, until the carrots are tender. Remove from heat and stir in the lime juice and cilantro.

Fluff the cooked rice with a fork and divide it evenly into four separate bowls; top each bowl with the curry. Serve hot.

note: Thai curry paste comes in the spicy red variety and the mild green variety. There is also a yellow curry paste, but it is more akin to an Indian curry. Curry paste can vary wildly with regards to its spiciness even within the same color. Taste as you go and add more if needed.

homemade squash ravioli w/ rosemary coconut cream

When I think of a meal to top all others in every aspect possible, homemade squash ravioli is what comes to mind. I first had homemade ravioli at a local wine tasting in my hometown of Palmer, Alaska. It had a butternut squash filling and was made by a *genuine* Italian chef. It was, to this day, one of the most incredible meals I've ever had, and I knew I had to make my own!

This ravioli is stuffed with a garlic acorn squash filling. Acorn squash is just so agreeable. Perhaps because it's not technically a menacing gourd but actually a relative of the causal summer squash. It's easier to cut open, you don't have to cube it and it cooks a whole lot faster than the banal butternut. To me, it's just as delicious, if not more so than its popular cousin. Drench this ravioli in a coconut cream sauce infused with fresh rosemary and you've got one show-stopping dinner.

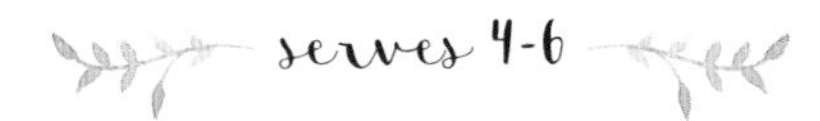

Squash

1 small (321 g) acorn squash

½ tbsp (7 ml) melted unrefined coconut oil

Pasta

2 cups (321 g) semolina flour

¾ cup (93 g) whole wheat or all-purpose flour

1 cup (240 ml) water

Filling

1 tbsp (18 g) vegan stick butter

½ medium (147 g) yellow onion, diced

2 large (10 g) garlic cloves, minced

⅓ cup (80 ml) coconut milk or soy milk

¼ tsp kosher salt

¼ tsp ground black pepper

2 tbsp (9 g) large-flake nutritional yeast

Cream Sauce

1 (13.6-oz [403-g]) can of full-fat coconut milk

2 tbsp (15 g) all-purpose flour

1 tbsp (5 g) large-flake nutritional yeast

1 tsp fresh rosemary, minced or ¼ tsp dried rosemary

½ tsp kosher salt

¼ tsp ground black pepper

Preheat the oven to 425°F (218°C) and cut the squash in half horizontally. Scoop out the seeds to compost and brush the halves with coconut oil; bake for about 25 minutes, until fork tender. When done, remove from the oven and allow to cool slightly.

While the squash cooks, add the flours to a food processor with the dough blade attached and pulse a few times to combine. While the processor is running, drizzle in the water. The dough should collect into a large ball. On a lightly floured surface, form the dough into a ball and cleave it into two halves (about 324 g each). Cover with a tea towel (not terry cloth) and allow them to rest until ready to use.

Clean out the food processor. Heat the butter for the filling in a large cast iron skillet over medium-low. Add the onion and garlic; sauté about 5 to 8 minutes until fragrant and the onion turns translucent. Transfer to the food processor along with the remaining filling ingredients. When the squash is done baking, scoop out the flesh and add to the food processor, composting the skins. Process until the mixture is somewhat smooth and well combined. Alternatively, you could mash and stir the mixture together in a large bowl. Set aside until ready to use.

Bring a large pot of salted water to boil for the pasta. Add the cream sauce ingredients to a small saucepan and whisk well to combine over medium-high heat; bring to a boil. Reduce to a simmer stirring occasionally until the sauce has thickened slightly, about 7 minutes. Remove from heat and set aside.

While the sauce cooks, roll out one of the pasta balls into a large square that's about 1⁄16 inch (1–2 mm) thick or as thin as you can get it. Place a row of filling dollops (about 2 teaspoons [10 g]) on the bottom half of the square, about 2 inches (5 cm) apart. Fold the remaining half of the pasta sheet over the dollops. I like to run my fingers through the "roads" to make it easier to see where I'm cutting. Using a pizza wheel (or a ravioli cutter if you're fancy), run cuts in between the mounds of filling. Press all four edges of each ravioli together to seal. It's okay if your ravioli isn't perfect looking. That's part of its homemade, rustic appeal! Repeat with remaining dough ball and filling.

Boil the ravioli gently for about 5 minutes, until it's floated to the top and is tender. You may have to do this in batches, or feel free to freeze half the ravioli. Carefully drain the ravioli so as not to break them and serve immediately with the cream sauce.

grilled veggie pitas w/ cilantro lime sauce

During the summer of 2015, the year this book was written, Alaska had record-setting heat. We're talking high 80s during the middle of June . . . *for weeks!* It was unprecedented. I was never able to relate to the folks in the Lower 48 who fervently avoided turning on their ovens during the swelter of the summer, until then. Indeed, this recipe was developed out of *necessity*. Our savior was the shiny, potbellied grill, which allowed us to cook up a large batch of delicious veggies.

If you don't have a grill, I've included directions for a roasted version. Feel free to add any vegetables you like in addition to the zucchini, bell pepper, carrot and sweet onion. Do note that you may need to steam any veggies, before roasting, that should require more time on the grill, such as potatoes. I pile the perfectly charred veggies atop a bed of baby kale layered on a toasted pita, then slather it all with a zesty cilantro lime sauce.

makes 4 pitas

Vegetables

2 medium (438 g) zucchinis, diced

2 medium (468 g) bell peppers, diced (any color)

3 medium (177 g) carrots, sliced in ¼ inch (6 mm) thick disks

1 medium (278 g) sweet onion, cut into half-moon slices

3 tbsp (45 ml) olive oil

Dash of freshly ground black pepper

Dash of kosher salt

Cilantro Lime Sauce

Juice from 2 limes, about 2 tbsp (30 ml)

¼ cup (42 g) raw cashews (see note)

2 (10 g) whole garlic cloves

2 tbsp (30 ml) olive oil

1 tbsp (6 g) large-flake nutritional yeast

1 tbsp (15 ml) agave nectar

½ tsp fresh ground chili paste or crushed red pepper flakes

1 cup packed (23 g) fresh cilantro

4 pitas (*not* the pocket kind)

Baby kale or spinach for serving (optional)

Start by preparing the coals if you have a charcoal grill. Once the coals are hot, place a large grill basket on the rack in the grill and cover with the lid. Preheat for about 5 minutes prior to adding the vegetables. Alternatively, if you don't have a grill basket, chop the veggies in somewhat larger pieces and grill them kabob style. Or just roast them in the oven at 420°F (215°C) for about 30 to 45 minutes, until tender. If using a gas grill, preheat the basket over medium-high heat for about 5 minutes prior to adding the vegetables.

While the grill heats up, add all the prepared vegetables into a large mixing bowl. Toss well with the olive oil, salt and pepper.

When the grill basket has been preheated, add the vegetables to the basket and cover the grill with the vented lid. The basket should be over medium-high direct heat. Grill for about 5 minutes, then stir the veggies, ensuring that you scrape the bottom of the basket. Cover and continue to grill for an additional 10 to 15 minutes. Stir occasionally and keep a close eye on the veggies to ensure they don't burn, as with any grilling expedition.

While the vegetables are grilling, add all the sauce ingredients to a blender and blend until smooth, about 1 to 2 minutes. Transfer to a small serving dish and set aside. When there's a few minutes left for the veggies, toast the pitas using tongs over a medium-low flame on the stovetop or grill for about 5 seconds each side. Or, zap the entire stack in the microwave for about 30 seconds. Set aside until ready to use.

When the veggies are done, divide them between 4 warmed pitas atop a small handful of baby kale and drizzle with the cilantro lime sauce. A little of the sauce goes a long way! Alternatively, you can stir the sauce into the vegetables.

note: If you don't have a high-powered blender like a Vitamix or Blendtec, it might be necessary to soak the cashews for 2 hours in boiling water prior to using them. Just drain them when ready to use, discarding the water. This will help to soften them, rendering a super-silky cashew cream.

broccoli & tofu pad thai

I fancy myself somewhat of a pad thai connoisseur. Pre-vegan days I would add shrimp to my noodles, which I now replace with tofu. The fish sauce is substituted with just a little extra soy sauce, and there you have it . . . the ultimate vegan pad thai. This noodle dish is one of my very favorite meals, *period.* It's so easy and nutritious, and just about one of the most flavorful meals around. However, there's no need to call for delivery from the local Thai place every time a craving hits! I confess, this is the biggest staple in our house alongside my White Wine "Clam" Linguine (page 97).

This recipe has been revised, countless times, to perfection. I love to add steamed broccoli for a healthy boost and a bit of fiber, or sometimes I'll add in some faux chicken strips if I'm feeling really fancy. Crushed peanuts, cilantro, green onions and mung bean sprouts top steamed broccoli and oven-baked tofu that mingles with rice noodles tossed in a homemade pad thai sauce. Once you make this vegan pad thai, you won't ever go in search of another recipe.

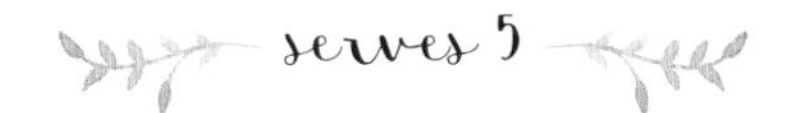

Pad Thai

1 (14-oz [397-g]) block firm or extra-firm tofu, drained and pressed

1 medium (215 g) head of broccoli, florets only

16 oz (454 g) pad thai rice noodles or sticks (sometimes called stir-fry noodles)

Sauce

½ cup (120 ml) soy sauce

½ cup (78 g) vegan brown sugar, lightly packed

¼ cup (60 ml) tamarind paste (see note)

¼ tsp garlic powder

Dash of crushed red pepper, to taste

Garnishes

8 medium (74 g) green onions, sliced on the diagonal

½ cup (10 g) fresh cilantro, chopped and lightly packed

½ cup (64 g) roasted peanuts, crushed

1 cup (60 g) mung bean sprouts (optional if they can't be found, see note)

Drain the tofu and wrap it in a couple of paper towels or tea towels (not terry cloth, the cloth used for bathroom towels). Place the tofu between two plates and stack a heavy object like a couple of large books on top. Allow the tofu to press for about 15 minutes. Of course if you have a fancy tofu press . . . please use the nonghetto version. Preheat the oven to 350°F (176°C) while the tofu is pressing.

When the tofu is done pressing and the oven is preheated, dice the tofu into small, bite-size pieces and arrange in an even layer on a baking sheet lined with parchment paper, silpat or coated with a nonstick cooking spray. Bake for about 30 to 45 minutes until golden brown.

While the tofu is baking, whisk all the sauce ingredients together in a small bowl and set aside. Prepare the green onions, cilantro, peanuts and mung beans; set aside. Cut the broccoli florets into bite size pieces. Steam the broccoli until bright green and just tender; about 5 minutes. Be careful not to overcook it! Cook the noodles according to the package so that they will finish cooking just after the tofu is done baking. Every package is different depending on the noodles and could take anywhere from 20 to 40 minutes to cook.

When the noodles are done cooking, drain them and return them to their pot. Stir in the sauce, tofu and broccoli over medium low heat. Kitchen tongs work well to incorporate everything. At this point you can mix in the garnishes or save them as a topping when serving. Once hot, remove from heat and serve steaming!

notes: Tamarind paste has eluded me in Alaska for several years. I've been unable to find it in our local grocery stores and just recently saw it was available at Amazon.com. If you're having a hard time finding it, use 2 tablespoons (39 g) tomato paste and the juice from 2 limes, about 2 tablespoons (30 ml).

Our stores stopped selling mung bean sprouts due to the risk of salmonella (umm, hello, with *that* logic, please stop selling chicken eggs), but they're incredibly easy to just sprout on your own. They also last *much* longer than the store-bought variety. Soak the beans overnight in water, then rinse twice a day for about a 3 to 7 days and voila . . . sprouts!

red wine minestrone w/ chard pesto

Mundane minestrone packs its bag and embarks on an exciting adventure to Italy in this robust spin on the classic soup. Red wine infuses my hearty, vegetable soup that's served with a substantial dollop of chard pesto, which lends an intriguing, meaty complexity.

It's a wonderful, veggie-loaded soup that warms my bones throughout our frigid Alaskan winters. I deliberately created the pesto for this soup with chard, as opposed to basil, which can be difficult to find during the chilly months up here. This way I'm able to make it all year long. If you do have access to a bit of fresh basil, it's really lovely to add a small handful to this soup. This might seem like a complex recipe with many ingredients, but it's actually really very easy and ready in about 30 minutes flat!

serves 8

Soup

1 tbsp (15 ml) olive oil

1 small (163) yellow onion, diced

3 large (28 g) cloves of garlic, minced

2 medium (148 g) carrots, sliced

3 medium (146 g) stalks of celery, sliced

½ small (449) head of green cabbage, chopped

1 (14.5-oz [411-g]) can of diced tomatoes

1 (15-oz [425-g]) can of white beans, drained

1 cup (240 ml) red wine (see note)

2 cups (475 ml) vegetable broth

4 cups (950 ml) water

2 tbsp (30 ml) soy sauce

2 dried bay leaves

⅛ tsp ground black pepper

1 cup (98 g) spiral or elbow pasta, dry

½ cup (23 g) fresh basil, chiffonade (optional)

Pesto

2 cups (108 g) fresh chard, destemmed and rough chopped (see note)

¼ cup (60 ml) olive oil

¼ cup (37 g) pumpkin seeds

3 tbsp (16 g) large-flake nutritional yeast

2 tbsp (19 g) sunflower seeds

2 tbsp (20 g) walnuts

1 large (5 g) garlic clove

½ tbsp (10 g) red miso paste

½ tbsp (7 ml) soy sauce

1 tsp fresh lemon juice

In a large, heavy-bottomed soup pot heat the olive oil over medium. Stir in the onion, garlic, carrots and celery; sauté for about 8 to 10 minutes until the onion begins to brown, then stir in the cabbage.

Deglaze the pan with the diced tomatoes and the juice from their can. Stir in the remaining soup ingredients, excluding the pasta and basil. Bring to a boil over high heat, uncovered, stirring occasionally.

While the soup is working up to a boil, add all the pesto ingredients to a food processor and process until very smooth, about 1 to 2 minutes; stopping to scrape the sides as needed. Set aside.

When the soup is boiling, stir in the pasta and reduce to a low boil. Cook for about 10 minutes, uncovered, until the pasta is al dente; stirring occasionally. Remove from heat and stir in the basil. Fish out the bay leaves with a slotted spoon (or just take care not to eat them).

Serve hot with a dollop of pesto in each bowl. Alternatively, you could stir all the pesto into the entire pot of soup.

notes: Any alcohol from the red wine is mostly burned off during the cooking process. However, feel free to substitute it with additional water.

Kale or spinach can be used in place of the chard.

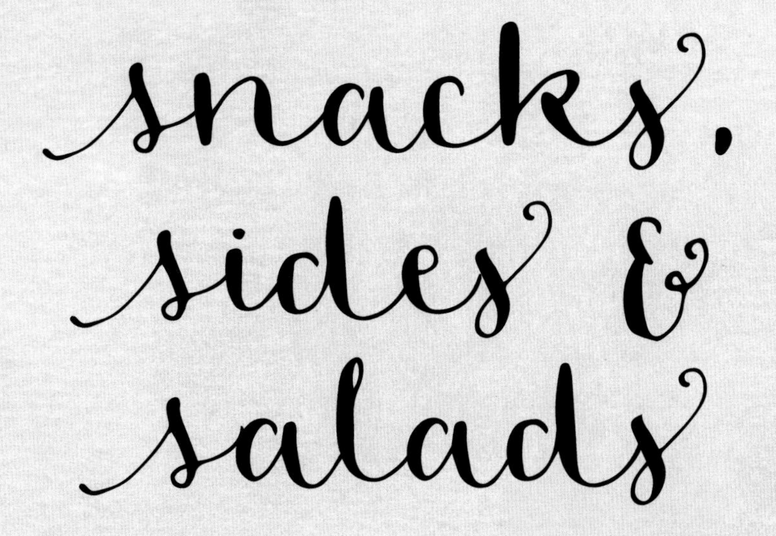

rumbling stomach quellers, meal copilots and crowd-pleasers

Sometimes I need a little something to quell a rumbling stomach and cure a surprise bout of *hanger*. Sometimes my main meal needs a copilot; not every dish is equipped to flying solo, you know. And sometimes a bowl of mixed vegetables sounds a whole heck of a lot better than a processed vegan hot dog. If you can relate to any of these statements, you've landed on a most appropriate chapter.

Snacks like my Collard Hummus (page 113) and Vegan Queso Dip (page 117) are crowd-pleasers and just the thing to bring to a party or enjoy as an appetizer. Miso & Horseradish Mashed Potatoes (page 133) or Fragrant Spanish Rice (page 118) are perfect accompaniments to main dishes like veggie meatloaf or enchiladas. Let's not forget the salads! No wimpy green salads here, folks. Goodness knows we get enough of them at any social function. In the following pages you'll find recipes for an amazing Summer Macaroni Salad (page 130), My Dad's Italian Pasta Salad (page 110) and a scrumptious Heirloom Tomato & Fresh Mint Millet Salad (page 126). Craft them into a light meal or partner with another dish for a feast.

my dad's italian pasta salad

Growing up, summer's arrival was excitedly trumpeted with this pasta salad. My dad used to make it *all the time* and I knew it had to have a place in this cookbook. While he was on the road I called him up to tell him I'd like to share his recipe with the world. I asked if I could please have his renowned pasta salad recipe and he told me, "Well that's the trouble . . . it's in my *brain*." He gave me as precise a recipe as he could over the phone (which really ended up just being an ingredient list), so I have mostly improvised.

This pasta salad should probably be called "Katie's Italian Pasta Salad," but I'd like to keep the name as a nod to my father. He likes to add pepperoni to his salad, but we omit that in my version. I prefer my substitutions of Kalamata olives to lend that salty bite and a homemade Italian dressing steps in to replace the Parmesan-laden store-bought variety (see note). Maybe I'll end up converting him to my vegan version in due time? Then we'll have to call it "Katie's Italian Pasta Salad" and it will be my charge.

serves 8

Salad

17.6 oz (500 g) spiral or bow-tie pasta, dry

1 medium (212 g) head of broccoli, florets only and chopped small

1 pint (255 g) (2 ½ cups) cherry tomatoes, halved

1 medium (155 g) red bell pepper, diced small

½ medium (114 g) red onion, thinly sliced in half moons

Scant ½ cup (60 g) pitted Kalamata olives, minced (see note)

Dressing

¾ cup (180 ml) olive oil

¼ cup (60 ml) apple cider vinegar

2 large garlic cloves, minced

2 tbsp (30 ml) water

1 tbsp (15 g) vegan granulated sugar

1 ½ tsp (7 g) table salt

¼ tsp ground black pepper

¼ tsp onion powder

Bring a large pot of salted water to boil for the pasta. Add the pasta to the boiling water and cook until al dente, usually about 8 minutes or so; consult the package. Drain, rinse under cold water and set aside.

While the pasta is cooking, steam the chopped broccoli for about 5 minutes until it turns a vibrant green and is just barely tender. Do not fully cook the broccoli; it should still be somewhat crunchy. Rinse the broccoli under cold water and set aside. Alternatively, it can be blanched by cooking in boiling water for 3 minutes then rinsing under cold water.

While the pasta and broccoli are cooking, whisk together all the dressing ingredients in a small bowl or liquid measuring cup. When the pasta is done and rinsed cold, combine the pasta and the dressing together in a large bowl.

Add the broccoli and remaining ingredients. Stir very well to combine, pulling up any pooled dressing from the bottom of the bowl.

Chill the salad in the fridge for at least 15 to 30 minutes before serving. Serve chilled. This salad is even better the next day when the al dente pasta has soaked up any remaining dressing and the flavors really have had time to meld together!

notes: If you'd like, you can use a premade Italian salad dressing, but beware that most contain Parmesan cheese. The dressing is really easy to whip up, and the salad uses the entire amount made. I encourage taking the extra step to make your own while the pasta and broccoli are cooking.

Be sure to buy pitted Kalamata olives, or else you'll have to do the pitting yourself!

collard hummus

Hummus is kind of like spaghetti sauce and salad dressing: It's so easy to whip up and wildly inexpensive to make at home, it's a wonder why people buy it at all! Yet, no one other than me better understands that everything is a give and take proposition. I make my own bread, spaghetti sauce and salad dressing at home, so more often than not I end up buying hummus from the store. If only time in the kitchen was unlimited!

However, this hummus packed full of leafy greens, sautéed garlic and onions is so good you'll never feel the need to purchase a tub of the stuff again. Hummus is definitely one of those items that is better homemade (I find most items are). Try it yourself and see how creamy, fuss-free and quick it is!

makes enough for a crowd (about 4-6 servings)

2 tbsp (30 ml) olive oil, divided

½ medium (158 g) yellow onion, diced

3 large (10 g) garlic cloves, minced

6 large (146 g) collard green leaves, destemmed and chopped

1 (15-oz [262-g]) can of chickpeas, drained and rinsed

¼ cup (60 ml) fresh lemon juice

1 tsp mustard, any type (see note)

½ kosher salt

¼ tsp paprika

¼ cup (60 ml) tahini

Pita chips, fresh pita bread or assorted veggies for dippin

In a large cast iron skillet, heat 1 tablespoon (15 ml) of the olive oil over medium. Add the onion and garlic; sauté about 3 to 5 minutes, until fragrant.

Add the collard greens and sauté about 8 to 10 minutes until wilted and bright green.

While the greens cook, add the remaining ingredients (except remaining olive oil), to a food processor. Process the mixture until smooth. When the collard greens are done, add them to the processor along with the onions and garlic. Process until smooth and creamy, about 3 to 5 minutes.

Transfer to a small serving bowl and drizzle on the remaining 1 tablespoon (15 ml) of olive oil. Serve with pita chips and/or an assortment of fresh veggies. Or, slather it on as a sandwich spread!

note: Mustard helps the nutrients in leafy greens—like collard, chard, kale and so on—be more bioavailable for absorption. I often add in about ½ to 1 teaspoon when I'm using leafy greens in a recipe. With such a small amount, no flavor is really detectable.

falafel & quinoa spinach salad

I love falafel, but I don't love the fact that it's cooked by *literally* bathing in a body of oil. They're such healthy little gems, it seems quite a shame to then subject them to a deep-fat frying; it's an insult to their nature. *Baking* them can sometimes result in a little drier and less crispy falafel but for everyday purposes I think it's a great compromise. However, if you feel inclined, I've included directions for frying as well.

I've created a healthy falafel that pairs with a protein-rich salad for a hearty meal. Baked, crispy falafel lays atop a bed of warm, quinoa and spinach dressed in a rich tahini sauce and studded with creamy avocado and fresh tomato. This is a nutritious and flavorful meal that keeps well and is delicious either hot or cold.

serves 4 / makes 8-10 falafels

Falafel

½ cup (10 g) fresh parsley leaves

¼ medium (71 g) yellow onion, rough chopped

1 (15-oz [425-g]) can of chickpeas, drained and rinsed

3 large (14 g) garlic cloves, minced

2 tbsp (15 g) all-purpose flour

1 tbsp (15 ml) ground flax seed

½ tbsp (7 ml) fresh lemon juice

2 tsp (2 g) ground cumin

½ tsp ground coriander

¼ tsp baking soda

¼ tsp ground black pepper

¼ tsp kosher salt

Dressing

¼ cup (60 ml) tahini

1 tbsp (15 ml) fresh lemon juice

1 tbsp (15 ml) agave nectar or maple syrup

½ tbsp (7 ml) soy sauce

Splash of water, if necessary

Salad

2 cups (475 ml) vegetable broth

1 cup (154 g) white quinoa, dry (see note)

1 medium (155 g) avocado, pitted and chopped

1 large (288 g) vine-ripened tomato, chopped

2 (10 g) green onions, sliced on the diagonal

6 cups (134 g) fresh spinach or baby kale

Preheat the oven to 425°F (218°C) if baking the falafel. In a food processor, pulse the parsley until chopped. Add the onion and pulse until chopped small. Add in the remaining falafel ingredients and process for about 10 seconds until well combined and a crumbled texture, but not so processed that it becomes a mush; scrape down the sides as needed.

To bake, divide the falafel batter into 8 patties on a baking sheet coated with a nonstick cooking spray. Wet your hands and shape them as you'd like them to be, because they won't change shape in the oven. Bake for 25 minutes, then flip them and rotate pan; bake an additional 25 minutes until golden brown on both sides. Remove from the oven and set aside.

If frying, heat 3 inches (7.6 cm) of oil to about 375°F (190°C) in a large pot. Form the batter into about 10 balls. To test, fry 1 ball for about 3 minutes per side, until golden brown. If it breaks apart, add a few dashes of flour to the remaining batter. Continue to fry as many balls as you can fit in the pot, until golden brown. Place them on a plate lined with a few paper towels.

While the falafel bakes, whisk together dressing ingredients in small bowl and set aside until ready to use. Add a splash of water to obtain desired consistency, if necessary.

Bring the vegetable broth and quinoa to a boil in a medium saucepan over high heat. Reduce to a simmer and cover; cook for 12 to 15 minutes. Remove from heat and allow to sit, covered, for 10 minutes. Fluff with a fork and set aside.

While the quinoa cooks, chop the avocado, tomato and green onions. When the quinoa is done, stir in the dressing until well incorporated. Then, stir in the remaining salad ingredients. The warm quinoa should slightly wilt the spinach.

To serve, divide the quinoa and spinach salad among four plates and top each with falafel.

note: If using red quinoa, be aware that it takes a bit longer to cook. The directions included are for regular, white quinoa.

vegan queso dip

My husband, Todd, loves to buy those giant soft pretzels in bulk. They're delicious, of course, but even *more* delicious dunked into that neon-yellow nacho cheese sauce! You know the one. I'm not aware of any *vegan* queso available for purchase (especially up here in Alaska), so we make our own from scratch! That's essentially how this cheese dip got its roots as a staple in our kitchen.

Who says vegans can't have queso? You won't believe that a few potatoes and carrots could possibly make a nacho cheese sauce that is so creamy and rich. Green chilies and diced tomatoes are added for a zesty flair, but this cheese is great plain as well. Slather it over nachos, dunk chunks of soft pretzels into it or stir it into pasta shells—it's pretty terrific on anything and you can feel satisfied knowing that this queso is really pretty good for you!

serves 8

Cheese

3 medium (390 g) boiling potatoes (see note), scrubbed clean and diced

3 medium (150 g) carrots, sliced

½ cup (120 ml) water

½ cup (123 g) large-flake nutritional yeast

¼ cup + 2 tbsp (90 ml) olive oil

1 tsp chipotle chili powder or cayenne powder (optional)

1 tsp table salt

½ tsp garlic powder

½ tsp onion powder

½ tsp ground turmeric

Dash of ground black pepper

Add-ins

1 (4-oz [113-g]) can of minced fire-roasted green chilies

1 medium (85 g) roma tomato, diced small

Bring a large pot of water to boil. Add the diced potatoes and carrots. Boil, uncovered, for about 20 minutes or until the veggies are fork-tender.

While the potatoes and carrots cook, add the remaining cheese ingredients to a high-powered blender. When the veggies are done, add them to the blender as well.

Blend on medium power, partially uncovered to allow the steam to vent. If you have a tamper, *use it!* Potatoes can be hard work for a blender, so you might need to allow the blender to take a break halfway through blending. If you don't have a high-powered blender, mash the potatoes and carrots first before adding them to the blender.

Once super smooth, stir in the chilies and tomato. Serve hot. Store any leftovers in the fridge and consume within a few days.

notes: Any low starch potato such as waxy, fingerling, baby reds or creamer potatoes will work well. Avoid using high-starch potatoes like russets.

If you don't have a high-powered blender, a food processor might do the trick. A couple of times my Vitamix has actually shut itself off while blending up this recipe. It says right in the manual that potatoes are very laborious for the blender to work with. If it shuts off, it's probably okay. Let it cool down for about 5 to 10 minutes before resuming blending.

fragrant spanish rice

I love a Spanish rice filled with tasty veggies like sautéed bell pepper, garlic and onion. Aromatic spices and herbs like chili powder, oregano, paprika and cumin infuse this fragrant jasmine rice with a zesty kick. Spanish rice is a most unusual craving of mine and I frequently find myself yearning for it! There's not a lot of really great Mexican or Spanish joints up here in Alaska (go figure), so I almost always ending up winging it at home.

This rice makes a wonderful side dish of course, but Todd and I like to stuff it in a pita with a bit of lettuce and some vegan shredded cheese for a pita-taco hybrid! Any way you dice it, this is a two-pot wonder that's done in about 45 minutes flat.

serves 6

Aromatics

1 tbsp (15 ml) olive oil

1 medium (140 g) red bell pepper, diced small

1 medium (270 g) yellow onion, diced small

3 large (16 g) garlic cloves, minced

2 tsp (5 g) chili powder

1 tsp dried oregano

1 tsp ground cumin

½ tsp salt

¼ tsp paprika

1 ½ cups (309 g) jasmine rice, dry (see note)

1 (15-oz [425-g]) can of tomato sauce

2 cups (475 ml) water

1 cup (240 ml) vegetable broth

In a cast iron skillet or heavy-bottomed soup pot, heat the oil over medium. Add the remaining aromatic ingredients; sauté for about 10 minutes, until the onion begins to brown.

While the onion browns, rinse the rice under cold water to remove the starch. Add to an unplugged rice cooker along with the tomato sauce, water and broth. Do not stir.

Once the onion mixture is done browning, add it to the rice cooker and stir until just combined. Plug in the cooker and cook until it signifies the rice is done, about 30 minutes. Test a few pieces of rice. If the rice isn't quite tender yet, stir the mixture and cook again until the rice is fully cooked. If you have to stir it a few times, that's okay.

Alternatively, the rice can be cooked via the stovetop by browning the onions in a heavy-bottomed soup pot. Add the remaining aromatic ingredients along with the tomato sauce, water and broth; bring to a boil over high heat. Stir in the rice and reduce to a simmer; cook, covered, for about 20 to 25 minutes. Do not remove the lid during this time. Once the time is up, check the rice for doneness. If it needs more time, cover and continue to cook. Once done remove from heat and allow to rest, covered, for 5 minutes.

Serve hot as a side, in a burrito or stuffed into a taco!

note: I like to use jasmine rice because of its aromatic quality and fast cooking times. If using different rice, the water ratio and cooking time may need to be adjusted.

wild rice & spinach salad w/ tempeh

This is a great side, but can definitely hold its own when it comes to the makings of a hearty meal. There's something so rustic and unique about wild rice. It doesn't make its way into my diet very often, probably due to its extended cooking time, but I find it to be such an invigorating departure from the usual jasmine rice I use. I positively delight in the nutty flavor and chewiness of wild rice.

In this salad, fresh spinach is wilted slightly by pan-fried tempeh, wild rice and sautéed mushrooms. It's dressed in a creamy, balsamic vinaigrette and topped with crunchy sunflower seeds. You can feel good about this protein-packed, whole-food meal that's sure to satisfy.

serves 4

1 ½ cups (350 ml) vegetable broth

½ cup (91 g) wild rice, dry

¼ cup (60 ml) olive oil, divided

4 large (164 g) cremini mushrooms, sliced

2 large (10 g) garlic cloves, minced

1 (8-oz [227-g]) package tempeh, cut into medium triangles

5 oz (142 g) fresh spinach, washed and dried

1 tbsp (15 ml) balsamic vinegar

1 tsp fresh oregano or ¼ tsp dried oregano

2 tbsp (6 g) fresh parsley

½ tsp kosher salt

¼ tsp black pepper

2 tbsp (15 g) sunflower seeds (see note)

In a rice cooker, combine the vegetable broth and the rice. Cook according to your rice cooker; about 1 hour or until the cooker alerts you that the rice is done. If cooking the rice via stovetop, combine the vegetable broth and rice in a medium saucepan; bring to a boil over high heat. Reduce to a simmer and cook, covered, for about 50 minutes until the rice is tender. Drain off any excess liquid.

While the rice cooks, heat 1 tablespoon (15 ml) olive oil in a large cast iron skillet over medium. Sauté the mushrooms and garlic for about 10 minutes, until the mushrooms are shrunken, dark in color and most their liquid has evaporated. Transfer to a large serving bowl and set aside.

Add an additional 1 tablespoon (15 ml) olive oil to the skillet and heat over medium. Arrange the tempeh triangles so they aren't overlapping and brown for 5 minutes; flip and brown an additional 5 minutes. Once done browning, cut into bite-size pieces if you like.

While the tempeh browns, add the fresh spinach to the mushrooms. In a small bowl or liquid measuring cup, whisk together the remaining 2 tablespoons (30 ml) of olive oil, balsamic vinegar, herbs, salt and pepper. Add half the dressing to the spinach and stir well to coat.

Add the cooked rice, browned tempeh and sunflower seeds to spinach mixture. Top with the remaining dressing and stir well to combine and coat everything.

Serve warm or chilled.

note: Feel free to use pepitas, sesame seeds, almonds, pistachios or any other nut and/or seed you'd prefer in place of the sunflower seeds.

skillet green beans & roasted potatoes

Sometimes the simplest side dishes are often the best. Home-style cut russet potatoes, roasted until crisp and golden are one of the most comforting foods around. I'm not a huge fan of green beans (it's a texture thing), so sautéing them is about the only way I really enjoy the lanky beans. If you've got haricots verts haters in your family, this wholesome recipe is for you!

Crispy, roasted potato fries and skillet-sautéed green beans mingle with fresh parsley, sprinkled with a light seasoning for a healthy side dish. This is a perfectly elementary, yet comforting addition to any meal that even the pickiest of eaters will enjoy!

serves 4

Potatoes

3 medium (739 g) Russet potatoes, thick julienned (see note)

1 tbsp (15 ml) olive oil

½ tsp kosher salt

¼ tsp ground black pepper

¼ tsp onion powder

Green Beans

½ tbsp (7 ml) olive oil

8 oz (240 g) fresh string green beans, trimmed

2 (9 g) garlic cloves, minced

3 tbsp (9 g) fresh parsley

Preheat the oven to 400°F (204°C). Scrub the potatoes clean and dry very well. Add the cut potatoes to a large mixing bowl. Drizzle with 1 tablespoon (15 ml) olive oil and add the salt, pepper and onion powder. Stir well to coat evenly.

Spread out the potatoes into a single layer on a large baking sheet lined with parchment paper or silpat. Roast for about 45 minutes, flipping them halfway through.

Wait until the potatoes are halfway done roasting (about 20 minutes in) to prepare the green beans. Heat ½ tablespoon (7 ml) olive oil in a large cast iron skillet over medium. Add the green beans and sauté for about 15 to 20 minutes until tender, stirring occasionally. When there's about 3 minutes left for the beans to cook, add in the garlic and sauté until fragrant and slightly golden; about 3 minutes.

Gently toss the roasted potatoes, sautéed green beans and fresh parsley together in a large serving bowl. Serve warm.

note: It's important to use a medium- to high-starch potato for this dish. An all-purpose Yukon Gold potato would be a nice alternative to the Russet, but avoid using fingerling or new potatoes.

roasted fingerling potatoes over baby greens w/ stone-ground mustard vinaigrette

If you allow me, I'll confess something that dare I say is pretty much sacrilegious in the vegan world. Okay, here goes it . . . *I'm not a green salad person.* I know. It's not that I don't *like* salads or leafy greens in general. *I do* . . . I'd just rather eat spinach stirred into soup, kale baked into lasagna and raw veggies wrapped up in a summer roll.

That being said, I adore this salad. It's about the *only* green salad you'll find in this cookbook. Not a stereotypical vegan cookbook, huh?! Congratulations, we're breaking molds here, people.

This simple and easy salad is composed of crispy, roasted fingerling potatoes on a bed of fresh baby greens drizzled with an herbed, sweet and tangy mustard dressing. A fabulous side dish or a wonderfully light meal for dinner that will spread a smile across those salad haters' faces.

serves 3 as a meal or 6 as a side

Potatoes

1 lb (450 g) fingerling potatoes, scrubbed clean and slice into coins

1 tbsp (15 ml) olive oil

1 tsp garlic powder

1 tsp paprika

½ tsp onion powder

½ tsp ground turmeric

¼ tsp table salt

Dash of ground black pepper

Vinaigrette

1 cup (240 ml) extra virgin olive oil

¼ cup (60 ml) red wine vinegar

2 tbsp (30 ml) stone-ground mustard (see note)

2 large (10 g) garlic cloves, minced

1 tbsp (15 ml) minced shallot or onion

1 tbsp (15 ml) agave nectar or maple syrup

2 tsp (2 g) dried oregano

2 tsp (2 g) dried parsley

½ tsp table salt

¼ tsp ground black pepper

Assorted fresh baby salad greens

Preheat the oven to 425°F (218°C).

Place the sliced potatoes in a medium mixing bowl along with the remaining potato ingredients and mix well to coat.

Coat a baking sheet with a nonstick cooking spray or line with parchment paper or silpat. Spread the potatoes out in an even layer and roast for 30 minutes, stirring the potatoes halfway through, until tender and slightly crispy. Transfer the potatoes back to the mixing bowl.

While the potatoes roast, add all the vinaigrette ingredients to a salad dressing bottle (or mason jar). Shake vigorously to combine.

Measure out ⅓ cup (80 ml) of the vinaigrette and stir into roasted potatoes to coat. Serve the potatoes over a bed of greens and topped with additional vinaigrette, to taste. If you have leftover dressing, store it in the fridge and consume within one week.

note: Stone-ground mustard can often be found near the deli section, if not with the other mustards. Dijon mustard may be used as a substitute.

heirloom tomato & fresh mint millet salad

This is such a lively, wonderful salad. It's an especially favorable choice when you *dread* encountering yet another quinoa and/or couscous salad. Millet is often cast aside for its trendier cousins, but here it proudly shines with plump heirloom tomatoes, toasted almonds, fresh mint and salty Kalamata olives. It's a perfect spring salad that's wonderful alone or stuffed into a pita. I make many variations of this salad, which is a staple in our home.

Quinoa or couscous will absolutely be acceptable substitutes in this dish, but I encourage branching out and using millet. I also love millet studded in my homemade sandwich bread, as creamy breakfast porridge and mixed into seeded cookies, so it's great to have on hand!

serves 4

Salad

1 cup (191 g) millet, dry (see note)

2 cups (475 ml) water

½ tsp kosher salt, divided

⅓ cup (57 g) almonds (or other nuts), chopped

1 cup (200 g) small heirloom or cherry tomatoes, halved then sliced

½ cup (18 g) fresh mint, chopped

½ cup (22 g) fresh parsley, chopped

10 (35 g) pitted Kalamata olives, finely chopped

Dressing

¼ cup (60 ml) olive oil

1 tbsp (15 ml) soy sauce

1 tbsp (15 ml) fresh lemon juice

1 tbsp (15 ml) agave nectar or maple syrup

Dash of ground black pepper

In a medium saucepan, toast the millet over medium heat for about 5 minutes. Toss every minute or so, until it becomes fragrant and browns slightly.

Add the water—be careful because it will sputter when it hits the hot pan—as well as ¼ teaspoon kosher salt. Stir and bring to boil over high heat; reduce the heat to low and cover. Simmer for 15 minutes, then remove from the heat and allow to sit for 10 minutes; fluff with a fork when done cooking.

While the millet cooks, toast the chopped nuts in a small frying pan over medium heat for about 3 to 5 minutes; stir every 30 seconds to ensure they don't burn. Once they are very slightly browned and fragrant, remove from heat, transfer to a small bowl and set aside.

In a medium serving bowl, add the tomatoes, mint, parsley, Kalamata olives and toasted almonds. Stir well to combine.

In a small bowl or liquid measuring cup, whisk together the dressing ingredients including the remaining ¼ teaspoon kosher salt. Add the millet and the dressing to the serving bowl and stir very well to combine.

Serve warm or chilled. This is fantastic alone or as a side dish. I like to stuff a bit inside a tortilla or pita coated with hummus if I'm super ravenous.

note: You can find millet in the bulk bin of your local grocery store. Millet can have a texture similar to quinoa and couscous (which is how I've used it here) or it can have a creamy, mashed potato or porridge-like texture with an extra bit of water and an extended cooking time. It sure is one versatile little fella!

fresh zucchini salad

I love the fresh crunch of this vibrant, tart summer salad. Crisp zucchini, crunchy bell peppers, sweet cherry tomatoes, salted Kalamata olives and briny capers all mingle together, awash with a homemade, herbed lemon dressing. If you need a separation from heavy foods, are embarking on a clean eating streak or just fancy yourself some seriously delicious whole foods; this salad has got your back. Eat it as a side, alone or stuff it into a pita for a complete meal.

serves 6

Veggies

2 medium (508 g) zucchini, spiralized or julienned

½ small (117 g) yellow onion, diced small

2 medium (206 g) bell peppers (any color), diced small

1 cup (171 g) cherry tomatoes, halved

⅓ cup (55 g) pitted Kalamata olives, minced

¼ cup (45 g) capers

Dressing

Juice from 1 lemon (about ¼ cup [60 ml])

¼ cup (60 ml) olive oil

1 tbsp (15 ml) agave nectar or maple syrup

1 tsp dried Italian herbs

½ tsp kosher salt

½ tsp ground black pepper

2 sprigs of fresh thyme, destemmed

In a large serving bowl, add the veggie ingredients and gently toss to combine.

Whisk the dressing ingredients together in a small bowl or liquid measuring cup and pour over the veggies; toss to coat.

Serve immediately and consume within the same day.

note: This salad can get a bit liquidy when the zucchini releases its juices as time passes. It's best served immediately, ensuring there are no leftovers.

summer macaroni salad

I didn't grow up eating casseroles, chili with Fritos, macaroni salad or even that green bean dish with the Funyuns on top; the foods that I think of as quintessentially *American*. It could just be an Alaskan anomaly, as we're separated from most of the United States by an entire, vast nation (hint, it's Canada). Are we just too removed to adopt such cultural food oddities? Perhaps it was simply my upbringing, but I suspect it's a native Alaskan thing as none of my friends shared these dishes with their families either.

Yet, this doesn't explain my inexplicable and utterly spontaneous cravings for macaroni salad. I'd only had the stuff a few times at random work functions or slopped as a side dish at some late-night restaurant before I had ever actually made it myself. Commercially prepared macaroni salad is *absolutely dreadful*, for sure, so I can't even imagine the origin of my hankerings.

My macaroni salad has just the right amount of sweet and tang to it. Not too much dressing, but definitely full of crunchy summer vegetables. It whips up in a breeze and will stand out from the sad and drowning macaroni salads of your nightmares, found at summer BBQs across the nation. The best part is that no one will guess it could *possibly* be vegan.

serves 6-8

Pasta

1 lb (454 g) elbow pasta, dry

¼ cup (60 ml) apple cider vinegar or white vinegar

Dressing

1 cup (237 g) vegan mayonnaise

Juice from 1 lemon (about ¼ cup [60 ml])

1 tbsp (15 ml) soy sauce

1 tbsp (22 g) mustard (I like stone-ground)

½ tbsp (7 g) vegan granulated sugar

1 tsp garlic powder

¼ tsp ground black pepper

Veggies

2 large (107 g) celery ribs, sliced

2 medium (241 g) roma tomatoes, diced small

1 medium (101 g) orange bell pepper, diced small

½ large (170 g) onion, diced small

¼ cup (10 g) fresh parsley, chopped

Bring a large pot of salted water to boil for the pasta. Cook the pasta about 1 to 2 minutes longer than recommended, about 10 minutes. It should be very tender (but not falling apart). Drain and transfer to a large serving bowl. Stir the vinegar into the cooked pasta and allow to rest for at least 10 minutes.

While the pasta cooks, whisk all the dressing ingredients together in a small bowl or large measuring cup. Set aside. Prep the veggies and add them to the cooked pasta. Pour the dressing on top and stir gently to coat.

Cover and place in the fridge to cool. Serve chilled . . . or warm, if you're like me and can't wait!

miso & horseradish mashed potatoes

I've always had a penchant for mashed potatoes with a bit of *flair*. I think I got it from my dad. These creamy (never gluey or lumpy) miso and horseradish infused mashed potatoes are a nod to him, the Mashed Potato King. At every holiday and major family function, my dad was the *only one* permitted to make mashed potatoes (well, maybe not *permitted*, but he made them so delicious that no one else dared to try to compete). Sometimes he'd make mouthwatering, garlic-infused mashed potatoes and other times he'd add horseradish for a spicy kick.

It's my great pleasure to report that this miso and horseradish blend got the King's approval. He did quip, as he dipped a second finger into the taters, ". . . they need butter." To which I squawked, "Dad! They have half a cup of it!" *Vegan butter ≠ butter*, in his opinion. He peered at me through a long pause and I stated very matter-of-factly, "You know vegan butter is pretty much real butter." He smiled slyly and seemed satisfied with that answer.

serves 6

- 7 medium (1.2 kg) whole Russet and/or yellow potatoes, scrubbed (see note)
- ½ cup (62 g) vegan stick butter
- 1 cup (120 ml) plain, unsweetened nondairy milk
- ½ tbsp (10 g) kosher salt
- 1 tbsp (14 g) red miso paste
- 1 tbsp (20 g) fresh horseradish paste, to taste (see note)
- ¼ cup (6 g) fresh parsley, chopped

Place the whole, unpeeled potatoes in a large pot and cover with 1 inch (2.5 cm) of water. Add a dash of salt and bring to a boil over high heat. Reduce to a low boil, cover and cook for about 30 minutes; until the potatoes are fork-tender. Drain and transfer the potatoes to an electric mixer. At this time you can peel the potatoes carefully with a potholder and a peeler or just leave them with their skins on, like I do. That's how I like my mashed potatoes. Plus the skins are good for you and tasty, too!

Once the potatoes are done cooking, melt the butter in the microwave for 30 seconds. Next, heat the milk in the microwave for about 1 minute and 30 seconds, until hot. Whisk the salt, miso and horseradish into the milk.

Beat the potatoes in a mixer on "stir" for 1 minute, until somewhat mashed. Add in the butter with the mixer still on "stir," then add in the milk mixture. Beat until it's reached its desired consistency.

Serve hot, garnished with fresh parsley.

notes: I like to use a combination of the very starchy Russet potato and the mildly starchy yellow potato. It makes for a very creamy texture. However, feel free to use all of one type or the other and be sure to try to obtain potatoes that are all around the same size, for cooking purposes. Stay away from using low-starch potatoes such as waxy, baby or red potatoes because they can result in lumpy mashed potatoes.

Horseradish paste can vary *widely* in its intensity and there's a great discrepancy between personal taste preferences for its spicy kick. Start with a little and add more if necessary, tasting as you go.

black bean & veggie quinoa salad w/ maple lemon dressing

This is one of my very favorite quinoa salads. I make many variations of the dish, but this one filled with sweet cherry tomatoes, fresh zucchini and protein-packed black beans is my go-to. I love the sweet, yet tart maple/lemon dressing that infuses the salad and ties all the flavors together. I could eat it for days on end! If you're looking for a super delicious salad that's packed with complete proteins with a hearty helping of veggies, look no further.

A fantastic "fridge cleaner" recipe, full of protein, nutrition-dense and it's ready in less than half an hour . . . that's a winning recipe, if you ask me!

serves 6

Quinoa

1 cup (178 g) white quinoa, dry

2 cups (475 ml) vegetable broth

Veggies

1 (15-oz [425-g]) can of black beans, drained and rinsed

1 heaping cup (196 g) cherry tomatoes, halved

4 small (391 g) zucchini, diced

2 medium (30 g) celery stalks, sliced

¼ cup (6 g) fresh parsley, chopped

Dressing

Juice from ½ a large lemon, about 2 tbsp (30 ml)

2 tbsp (30 ml) maple syrup

2 large (10 g) garlic cloves, minced

1 tbsp (15 ml) olive oil

½ tsp kosher salt

¼ tsp ground black pepper

1 tbsp (9 g) sesame seeds (optional)

In a medium saucepan, bring the quinoa and broth to a boil over high heat. Reduce to a simmer, cover and cook for about 15 minutes. Remove from heat and allow to rest, covered, for about 5 minutes; fluff with a fork and set aside.

While the quinoa cooks, prep the veggie ingredients and add them to a large serving bowl. Whisk together the dressing ingredients in a small bowl or liquid measuring cup and set aside.

When the quinoa is done, add it to the vegetables; stir in the dressing and sesame seeds, mixing well to combine.

Serve warm or chilled.

roasted veggie lentil salad w/ avocado balsamic dressing

This is a warm and comforting, protein-rich lentil salad that's a fantastic way to use up all those cherry tomatoes you've been wondering what to do with, not to mention the potatoes that are beginning to sprout and that avocado that's begging to be used before it exceeds its prime. Please tell me I'm not the only one this happens to!

Sweet, burst cherry tomatoes, roasted potatoes and wilted kale combine with earthy brown lentils and bathe in a tart, avocado balsamic dressing to make one hearty salad. I like to eat this as is, but it's also great piled high on a pita or as a side.

serves 6

3 cups (700 ml) water

1 cup (198 g) brown or green lentils, dry (see note)

1 tsp kosher salt

10 medium (412 g) fingerling or new potatoes, diced

1 medium (125 g) sweet potato, diced

1 ½ cups (270 g) cherry tomatoes, halved

2 cups (110 g) chopped kale, destemmed

Dressing

1 (110 g) ripe avocado, pitted and chopped

¼ cup (60 ml) water

¼ cup (60 ml) balsamic vinegar

2 large (10 g) garlic cloves

1 tsp kosher salt

1 tsp agave nectar or maple syrup

Dash of ground black pepper

¼ cup (9 g) fresh parsley, chopped

Bring the 3 cups (700 ml) of water to boil in a large saucepan over high heat. Stir in the lentils and salt. Simmer, uncovered, for 25 minutes or until the lentils are tender. Once done, they should retain some texture; drain and set aside.

While the lentils cook, preheat the oven to 415°F (212°C). Place the chopped fingerling and sweet potatoes in an even layer on a baking sheet coated with a nonstick cooking spray or lined with parchment paper or silpat. Drizzle with olive oil if you like, or leave naked. Set aside.

On a separate, rimmed baking sheet lined with parchment paper or silpat, arrange the cherry tomato halves in an even layer. Place both sheets in the oven. Roast the tomatoes for 20 minutes and the potatoes for 25 minutes or until tender, rotating the pans halfway through.

While the vegetables roast, place the chopped kale in a microwave-safe medium bowl. Top with plastic wrap or a plate, allowing a bit of steam to escape and microwave for 2 minutes on high or until the kale is wilted, bright green and slightly tender. Drain off excess liquid and place the kale in a large serving bowl.

In a blender, combine the dressing ingredients and blend on high until smooth, about 30 seconds. Add the dressing, lentils, roasted vegetables and parsley to the kale and stir well to combine.

Serve warm.

note: I don't advise using any split lentils or red lentils in this recipe as they aren't firm enough and tend to break down easily. Brown, green or black lentils will work beautifully.

bakery

irresistible sweet and savory goodies and breads

Where would this world be without delectable baked goods? Just imagine the prominent, mouth-watering aroma that hits you when you step into your local bakery, filled with fresh goodies just for you. Now envision that in your home. You're only pages away! There's something about a bakery item that's a bit more casual than dessert, more defensible. It's considerably more widely accepted to, say, eat a bagel or a muffin every day than a slice of pie or a brownie. Apparently such a thing is frowned upon by some people, though I confess, I can't imagine why.

Get your daily fix here with my Sweet Potato & Hard Apple Cider Bagels (page 155), a most appropriate autumn munchable. Sweet Ginger Banana Bread (page 143) makes for a luxurious breakfast or a divine pick-me-up. Roasted Garlic & Kalamata Olive No-Knead Bread (page 153) and my Foolproof Homemade Sandwich Bread (page 149) are weekly staples for my gluten-loving husband. Ah, but my favorite? The Garden Rhubarb & Candied Ginger Cream Scones (page 147) are *heaven* in a flaky and buttery, sugar-coated triangle.

Whatever you're looking for, whether it's sweet or savory, there's a homemade bakery fresh little somethin'-somethin' here for you and your family. And yes, you'll probably have to hide the bread, scones, muffins and so on, so they aren't all gobbled up in one sitting. I'm only slightly ashamed to admit that Todd and I eat an entire loaf of the sandwich bread the day we make it. It's irresistible; that's why the recipe makes two loaves.

wild blueberry pie chia jam

I love jam and really enjoy making my own quick, homemade jam. I've made several different chia jams and I wanted to love each one but just couldn't get over the odd texture from the whole chia seeds. "This isn't jam . . . " I would grumpily think to myself. That is until I decided to use *ground* chia seeds! Why hadn't I thought of that earlier?

What a game changer! The texture is perfect; silky and smooth with bits of berries, just how a luscious jam should be. This tart jam acquires a resemblance to blueberry pie (and a dose of antioxidants) with the addition of cinnamon, ginger and cloves. There's no canning required, whew, and it takes only 7 minutes to cook. I make a new batch about every week!

makes a little over 1 cup (240 ml)

2 cups (228 g) frozen wild blueberries (see note)

¼ tsp ground cinnamon

¼ tsp ground ginger

¼ tsp ground cloves

1 tbsp (11 g) ground chia seed (see note)

1 tbsp (15 ml) maple syrup

1 tbsp (15 ml) fresh lemon juice

Add the blueberries and spices to a small saucepan. Bring to a gentle boil over medium heat, stirring occasionally and mashing the berries with the back of a wooden spoon. The cooking time should be about 7 minutes.

While the jam is cooking, grind the chia seeds for about 1 minute, until it's powdery and no whole seeds remain. I just use a spare coffee grinder—the same one I use to grind my flaxseed!

Once boiling, remove from heat and whisk in the remaining ingredients. Be sure to use a whisk to incorporate the ground chia or else it will form chia clumps.

Pour into a small mason jar and allow to cool at least 30 minutes or until it's room temperature, before covering securely with a lid and placing in the fridge. Consume within 1 to 2 weeks.

notes: Feel free to use frozen raspberries or blackberries, or even chopped up strawberries. Fresh berries can be used, but take note that they'll require a shorter cooking time, about 4 minutes.

I've never found preground chia seed, but it's very easy to grind your own using a spare coffee grinder.

sweet ginger banana bread

If you're looking for banana bread that boasts bold banana flavor, look no further! This bread epitomizes all things banana thanks to the genius idea of *microwaving* the bananas, which helps to remove their liquid. Then, that liquid is reduced to super concentrate the flavor and it's added *back* to the bread. Thank you, America's Test Kitchen!

Crystallized ginger chunks stud this bread, which is sweetened with only bananas and dates! Coconut oil and ground flaxseed make a nutritious and cruelty-free substitution for the usual butter and chicken eggs. When friends and family ask you for the recipe, they'll be shocked to find the omission of sugar, butter and eggs! Take my word that this is the only banana bread recipe you'll ever want to make!

makes 1 loaf

2 tbsp (14 g) ground flaxseed

¼ cup (60 ml) cold water

5 medium (498 g) super ripe, spotted bananas, peeled and sliced

1 ¾ cups (209 g) all-purpose flour

1 tsp baking soda

½ tsp table salt

¼ cup (32 g) + 1 tbsp (5 g) crystallized ginger, minced and divided (see note)

8 (115 g) medjool dates, pitted and halved (see note)

½ cup (110 g) solid, unrefined coconut oil

1 tsp vanilla extract

Whisk the ground flax and the water together in a small bowl. Set aside until ready to use.

Place the sliced bananas in a large, microwave safe dish. Cover with plastic wrap and poke three slits in the plastic; microwave on high for 5 minutes. Place the cooked bananas in a fine mesh strainer over a medium bowl. Allow them to sit, straining for about 10 to 15 minutes, while stirring occasionally.

While the bananas strain, whisk the flour, baking soda and salt together in a large mixing bowl. Stir in ¼ cup (32 g) of the ginger, reserving the 1 tablespoon (5 g). Set aside until ready to use.

Add the dates, oil, vanilla and flax mixture to a food processor along with the strained bananas; process until the dates are smooth, about 3 to 5 minutes.

Preheat the oven to 350°F (177°F) and coat an 8 ½ x 4 ½-inch (21.6 x 11.4-cm) bread pan with nonstick cooking spray.

Transfer the banana liquid into a small saucepan and heat over medium-high for about 5 minutes, until it's reduced to about ¼ cup (60 ml). Add the juice to the food processor and pulse to combine.

Stir the wet mixture into the dry mixture until just combined. A few streaks of flour are okay, you don't want to over mix. Pour the batter into the bread pan and sprinkle the top with the remaining 1 tablespoon (5 g) ginger.

Bake for about 1 hour, until a wooden toothpick inserted into the center comes out clean. Rest in pan for 15 minutes, then remove from the pan and allow the loaf to rest on a wire cooling rack until almost completely cooled.

notes: Crystallized ginger, or candied ginger, can be found in the bulk section of the grocery store. It's one of my very favorite spicy snacks! I keep a small jar at my work desk and at home to ward off bouts of nausea. I never travel by plane or boat without the stuff!

If your medjool dates are a bit old and aren't very soft, they can be soaked in hot water and drained prior to use. No dates? Three-forths cup (130 g) of brown sugar can be used instead.

nordic seeded crispbread

This bread, more like a cracker, is a staple in Scandinavian countries. I was inspired to make my own version while happily munching away on the rye Wasa crackers found in our local grocery store. The Wasa crackers are crisp, large, crackling crackers made almost entire of rye flour.

This version, however, is loaded with good-for-you seeds, flax, millet and oats. Todd and I call my crispbread "Neckle Bread." Somehow, from the Norwegian word for crispbread (knekkebrød) pronounced "kin-ek-ee-bruh" I managed to pull out "Neckle Bread" and it just stuck! Try out this delicious and hearty Neckle Bread for yourself, it really couldn't be easier! It's the perfect light breakfast with a slathering of homemade jam and a hot cup of coffee. Or, as a snack, load it up with hummus and sprouts.

makes 18 crackers

1 cup (125 g) dark rye flour (see note)

½ cup (96 g) steel cut oats, dry

¼ cup (45 g) millet, dry

¼ cup (40 g) whole flaxseed, ground slightly (see note)

¼ cup (39 g) sunflower seeds

¼ cup (35 g) sesame seeds

¼ cup (35 g) pepitas

½ tsp table salt

1 cup (240 ml) water

Preheat the oven to 350°F (177°C).

Whisk all the ingredients together, excluding the water, in a large mixing bowl. Slowly pour in the water, stirring with a wooden spoon until it forms a thick dough.

Transfer the dough onto a baking sheet lined with parchment paper. Spread the dough out thin and even out with the back of the wooden spoon or spatula to form a 12 x 12-inch (30 x 30-cm) square.

Using the back of a spatula or a pizza cutter, score the dough into 18 pieces total (3 x 6 inch [7.6 x 15.2 cm] pieces), or as many as you'd like. This will make it easy to break apart once it's baked.

Bake for 1 hour, rotating the pan halfway through, until slightly golden brown and firm. Allow to cool completely before breaking apart.

Serve with fresh jam, slices of fruit, roasted veggies, hummus or a bit of baked tofu. Store in an airtight container.

notes: Whole wheat or all-purpose flour can be swapped for the rye flour if absolutely necessary. Light rye flour will work as well if the darker version is unavailable.

Flaxseeds left whole aren't digestible. Instead of completely pulverizing them, I whiz them in my grinder for a few pulses so they are only slightly ground. If you don't have a grinder, feel free to use either whole or ground flaxseed.

Feel free to add in any variety of seeds and/or nuts you like!

garden rhubarb & candied ginger cream scones

Rhubarb and candied ginger is such a stunning combination; two of my very favorite flavors marry in these beloved scones. And there is nothing more delicious than a cream scone! Angels will sing with one bite into these tart and sweet, melt-in-your-mouth scones.

A Christmas-like exhilaration overcomes me each summer as I tremble with the excitement of harvesting fresh rhubarb from the garden. It grows beautifully up here in Alaska and is one of the first plants ready for the picking. Rhubarb always makes me think of playing in the expansive garden as a child with my grandma, where she showed me how to wear the giant rhubarb leaf as a hat, but warned me not to *eat* the leaf because it's poisonous! It seems I was always trying to eat everything—and still am.

This recipe might seem long, but I assure you that these scones are really quite easy to make and pretty darn quick, too. They are the perfect lazy Sunday morning baking project that you can savor with a cup of coffee.

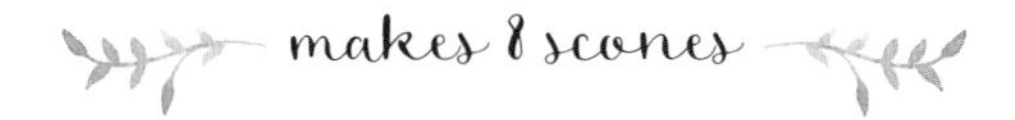

1 stick (113 g) chilled vegan butter, divided

½ cup (120 ml) plain, nondairy unsweetened milk

½ cup (120 g) vegan sour cream

2 cups (227 g) all-purpose flour

½ cup (116 g) vegan granulated sugar + additional for sprinkling

2 tsp (7 g) baking powder

½ tsp table salt

¼ tsp baking soda

½ cup (70 g) candied or crystallized ginger, minced (see note)

Scant 2 cups (207 g), about 5 stalks, fresh rhubarb, diced small (see note)

Grate all but 1 tablespoon (14 g) of the butter on a plate and place it in the freezer until ready to use. Place the 1 tablespoon (14 g) of nongrated butter in a small bowl and set aside. Whisk the milk and sour cream together in a small bowl or liquid measuring cup and place in the fridge until ready to use.

Whisk the flour, sugar, baking powder, salt and baking soda together in a large mixing bowl. Add the frozen, grated butter into the flour mixture, tossing with your fingers to incorporate and breaking apart any large clumps. Stir in the minced ginger. Make a well in the center and pour in the milk mixture, stirring until just combined.

Liberally flour a work surface and your hands. Turn the dough out onto the surface and knead about 8 times, until it forms a semi-ragged ball. Keep adding flour as needed to prevent sticking, as the dough is quite sticky. Roll the dough into a 12-inch (30-cm) square. Fold it like a business letter by bringing the bottom third up and folding the top third down over the bottom. Next, grab the left side and fold inwards, folding the right side over the left to form a perfect 4-inch (10-cm) square.

Place the dough square on a plate and put in the freezer for 5 minutes. Meanwhile, preheat the oven to 425°F (218°C). Melt the remaining 1 tablespoon (14 g) of butter in a small bowl in the microwave for about 10 to 20 seconds. Line a large baking sheet with a piece of parchment paper, silpat or coat with a nonstick cooking spray.

Remove the dough from the freezer and roll into a 12-inch (30-cm) square again, keeping your work surface dusted in flour. Evenly scatter the rhubarb among the entire square, pressing the pieces gently into the dough. Now, tightly roll the dough away from you into a 12-inch (30-cm) long log. Gently flatten the top with the rolling pin, so that it's about 4 inches (10 cm) high. Cut into 4 rectangles and then cut those in half diagonally. You should have 8 scone triangles.

(continued)

Transfer the dough triangles to the baking sheet. If they happen to be a bit wonky, reshape them as necessary. Coat with the melted butter, then sprinkle with a bit of additional sugar. Bake for about 20 minutes until the tops are just barely golden brown. Remove from the oven and cool on a wire cooling rack for 10 minutes.

Store in an airtight container and share with your friends and family for brownie points.

notes: Crystallized ginger or candied ginger can be found in the bulk section of the grocery store.

I don't recommend using frozen rhubarb, but if you must, be sure to thaw it out completely and then drain off as much excess water as possible. You don't want mushy scones!

The tip to perfectly flaky scones is to handle them as little as possible and keep the ingredients chilled.

foolproof homemade sandwich bread

I use this unfailing, memorized bread recipe every weekend to make two loaves of sandwich bread for my dear husband. There were many recipes that I made when I was learning to bake bread and I eventually just ended up with my very own, super-reliable recipe. It's a mish-mash of all the different things I learned from making bread every week and that I wish I'd learned sooner!

There's no way around the key to making a perfect loaf of bread. It's simply a lot of practice and a lot of patience. After a while, you just get to know what the dough should look like, how it should feel, when it's risen and been kneaded properly. It takes some time to acquire this skill, so keep at it! Think of all the money you'll save by making your own delicious, homemade bread. This looks like a long and overwhelming recipe, but I promise you it's really very easy and you'll have bread in three hours from top to bottom! Beginners are welcome here, so wash your hands and apron up. No excuses!

makes 2 loaves

1 cup (240 ml) warm water (110°F [43°C])

2 tbsp (30 g) vegan granulated sugar

2 tsp (7 g) active dry yeast

1 cup (240 ml) plain, unsweetened nondairy milk

2 tbsp (30 ml) olive oil

5 ½ cups (800 g) bread flour

1 tbsp (18 g) kosher salt

Vegan stick butter, to run over tops of loaves (optional)

Measure out the water, ensuring that it's the correct temperature. It should be hot, but not so hot that you can't hold your finger in it; think bath water temperature. Add the water to a large electric mixing bowl and whisk in the sugar until it's dissolved. Next, sprinkle the yeast on top of the water and stir gently with a wooden spoon until most of the yeast clumps are gone. Allow to rest for 5 to 10 minutes, until the yeast has formed a foamy blanket on top of the water.

In a microwave-safe liquid measuring cup, microwave the milk for about 60–90 seconds on high. It should be hot but not too hot to hold a finger in it, about 110°F (43°C). Add in the olive oil, no need to stir.

In a separate large mixing bowl, whisk together the flour and salt; set aside. Next, add the milk and oil mixture to the foamy yeast water. No need to stir.

Add one cup of the flour mixture at a time to the wet mixture, stirring with a wooden spoon until it forms a floury, shaggy ball. It might look quite dry, but it will come together when kneaded. If the ball is still a bit wet and there's no flour at the bottom, it may need more flour. It really just depends on the day and the weather!

If you'll be proofing (rising) the dough in the oven, go ahead and turn it on now to its lowest temperature. Once it finishes preheating, turn it off and open the door for a few minutes; then shut the door. Alternatively, you can proof it in a warm spot (at least above 75°F [24°C]), perhaps above the fridge.

Once the dough is well combined, attach the mixing bowl to an electric stand mixer. With the dough hook attachment, knead on speed 2–4 for about 8 to 10 minutes. Every couple of minutes, stop the machine and pull the dough off the hook, then turn the machine on again. I know it's a pain, but it's necessary. The dough should begin to try to worm its way out of the bowl as it becomes kneaded. It's hard to over-knead here, so if the ball isn't coming together add more flour, 1 tablespoon (7 g) at a time. After the time is up, the dough should be soft and smooth, not ragged at all. It should have the texture of your earlobe (really!) and not stick to the bowl. The bowl should be very clean, without any flour leftover or wet dough sticking to the sides.

Turn out the dough onto a lightly floured surface and knead the dough by hand about 10 times, just to finish it up. Coat the bowl with a nonstick cooking spray.

(continued)

Form the dough into a ball, with the top as taut as possible; place seam side down in the bowl. Cover the bowl with plastic wrap and place in a warm spot (above 75°F [24°C]) for about 1 hour or until it has doubled in size. I like to use my oven to proof. If the temperature is below 75°F (24°C), the dough will take longer to rise. Ideally, the proofing place is a bit warmer, around 80°F (27°C).

Once the dough has doubled, cleave it in two on a lightly floured surface and form each half into a ball. Be sure not to handle it too much; it doesn't need additional kneading and I don't punch it down. Allow the balls to rest on the counter, covered loosely with plastic wrap for 10 minutes.

Coat two 9 x 5-inch (23 x 13-cm) bread loaf pans with a nonstick cooking spray. Form the balls into loaves by rolling them out into two 9 x 9-inch (23 x 23-cm) squares. Fold the squares letter style by folding the bottom edge to the middle and then the top edge over the bottom one. Pinch the seams and sides closed and place them seam-side down in the pans. Cover with plastic wrap and place in the proofing spot again for their second proof; about 45 to 60 minutes or until the top of the loaves begin to rise just above the height of the pan (the entire thing doesn't need to dome over). The top of the loaf should be just a bit higher than the height of the pan itself. When there's about 15 minutes left to proof, carefully take the loaves out of the oven (if they are proofing in there) and preheat the oven to 425°F (218°C).

When the loaves have proofed and the oven is preheated, place the loaves side by side on the middle rack in the oven. Now, bring the oven down to 375°F (190°C) and bake for 30 to 40 minutes. The loaves, when done, should be just golden-brown on top and sound hollow when tapped. Carefully turn them out onto on a wire cooling rack and run a stick of vegan butter over the top a couple times for a nice sheen and a little extra richness. Allow the loaves to cool for at least 20 minutes before slicing.

To store, wrap the loaves in plastic wrap then in a cotton or linen dish towel (not terry cloth, the cloth bath towels are made of) or a plastic Ziploc bag, if you must. I store them in a cool place at room-temperature, with the sliced end down. Don't store in the fridge if you can help it.

notes: The yeast should foam up after 5 to 10 minutes. If it doesn't, then the yeast might be old or the water was too hot or perhaps too cold.

5 ½ cups (800 g) of flour is what I usually end up using, sometimes it's a little more or a little less. It just depends on the weather!

If you don't have an electric mixer, the dough can be kneaded completely by hand either on a lightly floured surface or pastry cloth, though it might take a bit longer.

If you have questions about this bread, please contact me on my blog at www.produceonparade.com. I'd love to help you in any way I can!

roasted garlic & kalamata olive no-knead bread

Briny kalamata olives and mouth-watering, roasted garlic are a delightful addition to this chewy, no-knead bread. *Exceptionally* easy to make; all one needs is a bit of time (hands-off time, of course). All it takes is basically roasting the garlic, mixing up the ingredients, dumping the dough in a bowl and letting it chill out for 12 hours. No kneading! Then proofing it for an additional 2 hours and baking. There is nothing better than digging into the sweet heaven that is fresh, homemade bread for a scrumptious, weekend lunch.

As a child, my family used to get kalamata olive rolls from a local bakery and the memory inspired me to develop a bread version. Plan to enjoy this bread about 20 hours from when you first start it. I like to start it Friday night. After I wake up Saturday morning and have had my coffee, I'll finish up the recipe and have fresh bread for lunch!

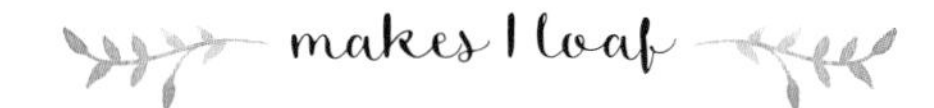

1 small (120 g) head of garlic

1 cup (160 g) pitted kalamata olives, chopped small

3 cups (426 g) bread flour or all-purpose flour

1 tsp dried oregano

¼ tsp instant yeast

1 ½ cups + 2 tbsp (147 ml) warm water

Preheat the oven to 400°F (204°C). Remove most of the papery shell on the outside of a small head of garlic; slice off the top, exposing the cloves inside. Place it face-side down on a small piece of parchment paper atop a baking sheet. Roast for 30 to 40 minutes, flipping halfway through. The cloves should be easily pierced with a knife when done. Remove from the oven and allow to cool for at least 10 minutes. Turn off the oven.

While the garlic roasts, chop the kalamata olives. In a large mixing bowl, whisk together the flour, oregano and yeast. Set aside until the garlic is done roasting.

To remove the cooled, roasted garlic cloves from the head, gently squeeze the bottom of the garlic head to pop them out; slightly mash the cloves. Add the mashed cloves and chopped olives to the flour mixture and stir well to coat them in flour. This will help keep them from sinking to the bottom of the bread.

Slowly stir the water into the flour mixture with a wooden spoon until well combined. Cover the bowl loosely with plastic wrap and place in a warm place for 12 to 18 hours to proof. The spot should be at least 70°F (21°C). The dough should be bubbly and have doubled in size when the time is up.

Next, scrape out the proofed dough onto a heavily floured tea towel (see note). Fold it over itself a few times. The dough will be very sticky, this is okay—you shouldn't be able to handle it too much. Cover it with plastic wrap and allow the dough to rest for 15 minutes.

Now, working quickly and with enough flour to keep the dough from sticking everywhere, form the dough into a ball. Turn the ball so it is seam side down. Cover loosely with another tea towel and allow to rest for about 2 hours. The dough should be doubled in size when the time is up.

When there is half an hour left for the dough to rise, place an oven safe and lidded, large cast iron, enamel, ceramic or soup pot (I like to use my dutch oven) in the oven and preheat to 450°F (232°C), without the lid on.

(continued)

When ready, carefully transfer the dough ball into the pot using the towels. Just plop it in, seam side up. Give the pot a few shakes to even out the dough if it didn't land quite evenly. It might look a little sloppy, but all will be well once it comes out of the oven.

Bake uncovered for 30 minutes, then cover with the lid and bake for an additional 15 to 30 minutes, until the top browns. Cool on a wire cooling rack and allow to rest for at least 10 minutes before slicing into.

Wrap it tightly in a cotton dishcloth to store.

note: Be sure to use cotton dishcloths when making this bread as opposed to terry dishcloths (the cloth that bath towels are made of). The terry fabric will cling to the dough.

sweet potato & hard apple cider bagels

Bagels always seem to conjure up good memories, don't they? As a treat, my mom would take us kids to the Alaska Bagel Factory to pick out three bagels to take home. I'd always choose spinach, blueberry and sweet potato. Since the Bagel Factory is over 50 miles away and one can never be too sure if the tops are brushed with egg, butter or what-have-you . . . I now make my own! *With a bit of a spin, of course.* That's the beauty of homemade bagels: the sky's the limit with creativity.

While perusing through the Vegetarian Flavor Bible, I saw that sweet potato goes well with apple cider. Much to my delight, I happened to have a hard apple cider hiding in the back of the fridge! It was decided that sacrificing it to the creation of a bagel was an honor. And so it was that these sweet potato and hard apple cider bagels were born. With a little pumpkin pie spice thrown in, it's an absolutely divine autumn breakfast and/or snack.

makes 8 bagels

½ cup (120 ml) hard apple cider (or regular apple cider/apple juice)

5 tbsp (75 g) vegan granulated sugar, divided + more for topping (optional)

2 ½ tsp (12 g) dry active yeast

½ cup (115 g) mashed sweet potato meat (about 1 medium sweet potato)

3 cups (350 g) all-purpose flour

1 ½ tbsp (11 g) pumpkin pie spice

1 tsp salt

1 tbsp (8 g) barley malt sweetener powder or syrup (optional)

In a microwave safe small bowl or liquid measuring cup, heat the apple cider in the microwave on high for about 1–1 ½ minutes. It should be about 110°F (43°C); warm enough to comfortably dip your finger in, but not so hot that you can't stand it. If it's too hot, allow it to cool for a minute or two.

Pour the cider into an electric stand mixer bowl and whisk in 3 tablespoons (36 g) sugar. Next, gently stir in the yeast with a wooden spoon until it's mostly mixed in. Allow to rest for 10 minutes, until a foamy blanket has formed. If this doesn't happen, most likely the yeast is too old or the water was too hot or too cold.

While the yeast does its thing, scrub clean a medium, whole sweet potato. Pierce it with a knife several times all over. Place it in a microwave safe bowl covered with plastic wrap and microwave for 3 minutes on high. Then, turn the potato over and microwave an additional 3 minutes. When done, slice in half lengthwise and allow to cool slightly.

While the potato cooks, whisk together the flour, pumpkin pie spice and salt in a medium bowl. When the potato has cooled slightly, scoop out ½ cup (115 g) of the meat and mash it very well with a fork. Whisk into the yeast mixture. Next, slowly add in the flour mixture, stirring with a wooden spoon. Once it's well combined and no flour remains at the bottom of the bowl, attach a dough hook to the mixer and knead for a good 10 minutes on speed 2–4. Stop to remove the dough from the hook every few minutes; this is important!

The dough is ready when it forms a soft mass, there is no more flour at the bottom and it's not sticking to the bowl too much. If it's still a bit wet, more flour can be added 1 tablespoon (15 g) at a time until it's no longer sticking to the sides.

Preheat the oven to as low as it will go; then turn it off and crack the door.

While the oven preheats, turn the dough out onto a lightly floured surface and knead by hand for about 3–5 minutes. It should be soft and feel like an earlobe. Form into a ball. Coat the electric mixing bowl with a nonstick cooking spray and place the dough ball inside. Cover with plastic wrap and place in the oven to proof for 1 hour or until it's almost doubled in size.

(continued)

Remove the dough from the oven and turn out onto a lightly floured surface. Cut the dough ball into 8 smaller balls; they should be about 4 ounces (96 g) a piece. Roll each one into a 6-inch (15-cm) long log and pinch the ends together to form a ring. I can't stress enough that you need to form the bagels exactly as you'd like to see them when they are all done. They will only rise very slightly. You don't want a giant, gaping hole in the middle but you also don't want the hole to be completely filled in. Allow the rings to rest for 15 minutes once shaped, covered loosely with plastic wrap.

While the bagels rest, fill a large soup pot with water until there's about 4 inches (10 cm) of water in the pot. Whisk in the barley malt and bring to a boil over high heat. Preheat the oven to 400°F (204°C). Place a wire cooling rack over a baking sheet and coat a different baking sheet with a nonstick cooking spray or line with parchment paper or silpat.

When the bagels are done resting and the water is boiling, carefully drop as many as you can fit comfortably (about four) into the water. Boil for 30 seconds on each side, flipping with tongs or a spatula. Fish them out using a fine mesh strainer. If you don't have a fine mesh strainer, a very large slotted spoon will work. Place the bagels on the wire cooling rack. Repeat with the remaining bagels.

After all the bagels have boiled, place them on the nonstick coated baking sheet and bake for about 24 minutes, until slightly golden. Flip the bagels over and rotate the pan halfway through.

Remove from the oven and allow to cool for at least 10 minutes on the wire cooling rack. At this point you can leave them naked or sugar coat the top. To sugar-coat them, place 2 tablespoons (24 g) of granulated sugar in a small, shallow bowl. Dip the tops in the water that was used for boiling them and then dredge in the sugar.

Store in an airtight container once cooled.

note: The barley malt sweetener powder is optional, but it's what gives bagels that certain "bageliness." It is also what colors the outside with the shiny, golden hue. I found mine at a local health food store, but if you don't have any, it can be omitted.

chai-spiced ginger muffins

These spectacularly chai-spiced, moist muffins are studded with oats and crystallized ginger for a rustic and complex flavor. I like to make these for special gatherings, *especially* during the autumn and winter months because they lend a certain festive appeal. However, they are so easy and delicious I could make them *every* weekend . . . all year long! These muffins are sure to become an everyday hit for your friends and family, too.

Sour cream might seem like an odd addition to a muffin, but it's what makes these so soft and scrumptious! These are a quick, super easy and wonderful way to cozy up with a cup of tea for the perfect breakfast and/or evening snack when there's a crisp chill in the breeze.

makes 12 muffins

Flax Egg

1 tbsp (7 g) ground flaxseed

2 tbsp (30 ml) cold water

Dry

2 cups (217 g) all-purpose flour

1 tbsp (15 g) baking powder

1 tsp ground cinnamon

1 tsp ground ginger

1 tsp ground cardamom

½ tsp table salt

¼ tsp ground cloves

Pinch of freshly ground nutmeg

Dash of ground black pepper

½ cup (75 g) crystallized ginger, chopped small (see note)

½ cup (45 g) old-fashioned rolled oats

Wet

¼ cup (57 g) vegan stick butter, melted and cooled slightly

1 cup (207 g) vegan granulated sugar

1 (12-oz [340-g]) tub of vegan sour cream

½ tsp vanilla extract

Whisk the flaxseed and water together in a small bowl. Place in the fridge until ready to use. Preheat the oven to 350°F (177°C).

In a large mixing bowl, whisk together the flour through and including the black pepper. Stir in the ginger and oats. Set aside.

In a large electric mixing bowl, beat the butter and sugar at medium speed. Add in the flax mixture, sour cream and vanilla; beat until well combined.

Slowly beat the dry mixture into the wet mixture at low speed until just combined. If there are sprays of flour, that's okay; be careful not to overmix the batter. It should be very thick.

Evenly distribute the batter into a regular muffin pan coated with a nonstick cooking spray or muffin liners. The batter should fill just about to the top of the liners. Bake for 30 minutes, rotating the pan halfway through, until the tops and edges are lightly golden-brown. Remove from the oven and turn out onto a wire cooling rack. Allow to cool for 5 minutes.

Store in an airtight container.

note: Crystallized ginger or candied ginger can be found in the bulk section of the grocery store. It's one of my very favorite spicy snacks!

Sugar

sweets

a variety of healthy, show-stopping and everyday treats

So, you've got a bit of a sweet tooth? Me, too. *Big time.* Forget the potato chips and pass me all the pies, please! Regrettably, I've been known to eat chocolate chips by the handful when I need a quick fix. However, I'd be comfortable saying that I lead a healthy lifestyle and love curating a wholesome, plant-dense diet. This doesn't mean that every now and again I don't indulge in some distinguished desserts, though. And yes, in a heartbeat, I'd live solely off my incomparable White Russian Tiramisu (page 187) and Divine Banana Cream Pie (page 172), if I knew such a diet could adequately sustain human life; there's no denying that.

You'll find some serious desserts in the pages that follow, but sometimes I like to incorporate a bit more *nourishment* when my unrelenting sweet cravings bluster in. That's why I've included recipes to help take the edge off a bit but still grant a clear conscience whilst indulging. Healthy desserts like Nutrition-Rich Brownies (page 175) and Spiced Rum Banana Pudding (page 163) will keep you guilt-free but utterly fulfilled in all things sweet.

Need dessert like yesterday? I've got you covered with my super-quick and elegant Cardamom & Clove Custard (page 167). If you're looking for a serious crowd-pleaser try your hand with one of my favorites like the Wild Blueberry, Rhubarb & Hazelnut Crisp (page 164) or my show-stopping Mocha S'more Pie (page 171). You'll find chocolate goodies, desserts bursting with berries, unique flavor combinations and many more recipes in between. There's definitely something here to delight everyone's taste buds and feed that sweet tooth.

spiced rum banana pudding

I absolutely love this little dessert. It's very quick, unbelievably easy and quite healthy with no refined sugars or oils. Packed with protein thanks to the silken tofu, it's a great way to get in an extra boost of the stuff. The pudding is sweetened with bananas and just a dash of maple syrup, a surefire way to cure my *aggressive* sweet tooth in a nutritious way. There's no doubt this gem will be a staple in your home as it is in ours!

serves 4

¼ cup (34 g) raw cashews, whole (see note)

3 medium (168 g) ripe bananas, divided and sliced

12.3-oz (349-g) silken firm tofu, drained (see note)

2 tbsp (30 ml) maple syrup or agave nectar

1 tbsp (15 ml) spiced rum (see note)

½ tsp vanilla extract

¼ tsp table salt

¼ tsp ground cinnamon

¼ tsp xanthan gum (optional, see note)

⅛ tsp ground cardamom

⅛ tsp ground turmeric (optional, for color)

Dash of freshly ground nutmeg

Place the cashews in a food processor and blend for a couple minutes until they are finely chopped.

Next, add 2 ½ bananas (saving half of one banana for the topping) and the remaining ingredients to the processor. Blend for about 3 minutes, until very smooth.

Divide into 4 small serving bowls and chill for at least 30 minutes. Serve chilled and topped with the remaining half of one banana.

notes: If you don't have a high-powered blender like a Vitamix or Blendtec, it might be necessary to soak the cashews for 2 hours in boiling water prior to using them. Just drain them when ready to use, discarding the water. This will help soften them, to render a super-silky cashew cream.

I like to use the shelf-stable Mori Nu brand of tofu that comes in a box as opposed to a plastic bin filled with water. It doesn't have quite as strong of a "tofu" taste to it. I buy a 12-pack from Amazon and it keeps for a very long time. Whatever tofu you use, it must be labeled "silken."

Feel free to add as much or as little rum as you wish. Leave it out for the kiddos.

The xanthan gum is totally optional, but it lends a velvety creaminess to this pudding.

wild blueberry, rhubarb & hazelnut crisp

Every fall, Todd and I excitedly take a mini backpacking trip a couple of hours east to a remote valley where we got married to pick mountain blueberries; the Prius gets packed with our large bags, Bailey the dog and vegan junk food. It's one of our most treasured traditions and it means we'll always have a few gallon-sized bags of blueberries in the freezer to last us throughout the year. Every time I pull the blueberries out of the freezer to use them in pies, jam or smoothies, I'm transported back to our joyful, blueberry backpacking trips.

Rhubarb grows beautifully in Alaska. Ready for harvest in early summer, it's such a nice addition to the usual boreal bounty that packs our freezer.

This is one of the easiest desserts to make. Bursting with wild blueberries and tart rhubarb, this sweet fruit crisp also features healthy additions like flaxseed, rolled oats and maple syrup for a wholesome flair. Baked in a cast iron skillet, it serves as a magnificent breakfast or a nourishing, scrumptious dessert.

serves 6

Berries

3 ½ cups (875 g) wild blueberries, frozen or fresh (see note)

1 ½ cups (375 g) chopped rhubarb, frozen or fresh

2 tbsp (13 g) ground flaxseed

2 tbsp (30 ml) maple syrup

1 tbsp (15 ml) fresh lemon juice

1 tsp vanilla extract

Crumble

½ cup (165 g) whole wheat white flour or all-purpose flour

½ cup (185 g) vegan brown sugar, packed

½ cup (156 g) old-fashioned rolled oats, dry

¼ cup (28 g) whole hazelnuts

2 tbsp (13 g) ground flaxseed

¼ tsp table salt

¼ tsp ground cinnamon

Dash of freshly ground nutmeg

¼ cup (70 g) chilled vegan stick butter, roughly chopped

Preheat oven to 375°F (190°C) and coat a 12-inch (30-cm) cast iron skillet with a nonstick cooking spray. In a medium bowl, combine the berry ingredients and mix well. A 9 x 9-inch (23 x 23-cm) baking dish can also be used.

In a food processor, pulse all the crumble ingredients, until the nuts are chopped small. Add the butter and pulse until the butter bits are no bigger than the size of a pea.

Evenly add the berry mixture to the skillet and cover uniformly with the crumble mixture.

Bake for 40 minutes, until the crisp is bubbling around the edges. I like to place a baking sheet on the rack below the skillet, just in case it bubbles over. Remove from oven and allow to rest for 5 minutes before serving. Serve warm.

note: If using frozen blueberries and/or rhubarb, don't thaw them prior to use.

cardamom & clove custard

I have a certain penchant for all things spiced with cardamom and clove; when combined, the two are an elegant pair indeed. If I hadn't thought of the name Produce On Parade, I think Cardamom and Clove would have been an exceptionally fitting name for my food blog!

This dreamy, silky soft custard is firmed up with a bit of coconut oil and spiced with the nostalgic scents of vanilla, cardamom and clove. I love how quick this is to prepare and it's refreshing to dive into a super protein-packed dessert. This custard is as easy and speedy as making a smoothie!

serves 2

1 (12.3-oz [349-g]) box of firm silken tofu (see note)

¼ cup (60 ml) melted unrefined coconut oil

¼ cup (60 ml) maple syrup or agave nectar

½ tsp vanilla extract

¼ tsp table salt

¼ tsp ground cardamom

Pinch of ground cloves

Drain the tofu of any liquid and place in a blender along with the remaining ingredients. Blend on low to combine everything, then increase to medium speed; blend for 1 minute.

Pour into two small bowls and place in the fridge, covered, for at least half an hour to set. Serve chilled.

note: I like to use the Mori Nu tofu that comes in a box and is shelf stable, as opposed to the kind that comes in the plastic bin. The tofu must be silken. It's creamy, as opposed to the type of firm tofu you'd use for a tofu scramble. It can be found at Amazon.com, but I buy mine at our local grocery store.

spicy cinnamon drinking chocolate

There's just something about drinking chocolate. It can be completely nostalgic, yet a little exotic and still utterly indulgent. This is *not* the hot chocolate or cocoa that you grew up with in America. This drinking chocolate is very thick and incredibly rich. It's consumed more frequently in other countries, like Italy and Spain, rather than in America and one can drink only a very *small* teacup of the heavy, molten chocolate.

My inspiration for this picante version, infused with cinnamon and cayenne, is from my *absolute favorite* spicy chocolate bar. I love sipping this drinking chocolate in the dead of the frozen winter, to warm my bones and comfort my soul. It's a winter weather necessity. Especially up here in Alaska!

serves 4 / makes about 1 cup (240 ml)

2 oz (56 g) unsweetened vegan baking chocolate, chopped small

2 cups (475 ml) cold, unsweetened plain nondairy milk, divided

Scant ¼ cup (40 g) vegan granulated sugar

¾ tsp ground cinnamon

⅛ tsp chipotle chili powder or cayenne pepper

Dash of salt

½ tsp cornstarch or arrowroot powder

½ tsp vanilla extract

In a small saucepan, heat the chocolate, 1 ¾ cups (240 ml) milk, and remaining ingredients excluding the cornstarch and vanilla over medium-low. Whisk continuously until the chocolate is melted. Be careful not to bring the liquid to a boil.

In a separate bowl, whisk together the remaining ¼ cup (60 ml) cold milk and the cornstarch. Slowly whisk into the pot. Whisk continuously over medium-low heat until bubbles begin to pop around the edge of the pot, about 3 to 5 minutes. The drinking chocolate should thicken slightly.

Remove from heat and whisk in the vanilla. Serve steaming hot in tiny cups or bowls.

notes: Use discretion when adding the sugar and the cayenne, to make the drink as sweet or as spicy as you like. Add more milk as needed to obtain desired thickness.

One serving is about ¼ cup (60 ml).

mocha s'more pie

When Todd and I were building our home, we cleared and leveled our own land and driveway (with *an unimaginable* amount of help from friends and family . . . Dad, I'm looking at you). It was a raw piece of land, so that meant we had to also clear for the gas and electric to come up our 800-foot-long driveway! It was a lot of work and we had many bonfires to burn the brush from clearing. Every time we set a pile of branches ablaze (when I wasn't chaining myself to every doomed birch tree), I'd yearn to grab my stash of vegan marshmallows, kick my feet up and do some roasting!

This pie was inspired by my ever-frequent s'mores daydreams. The toasted marshmallows create a stunning visual and the rich chocolate is poured into a hand-pressed graham cracker crust, reminiscent of a nostalgic s'more. I intensified the dark chocolate with a bit of coffee for even more "mmmmm" factor. My adult taste buds really respected this mocha inspired s'more pie, but feel free to leave out the coffee if you wish.

makes 1 (9-inch [23-cm]) pie

Crust

9 (139 g) vegan graham crackers

2 tbsp (30 g) semisweet vegan chocolate chips

1 tbsp (15 ml) vegan stick butter

3 tbsp (45 ml) canned, full fat coconut milk

2 (32 g) medjool dates, pitted and chopped

¼ tsp salt

Filling

2 cups (340 g) semisweet vegan chocolate chips

2 tbsp (30 ml) vegan stick butter

1 ¼ cups (295 ml) canned, full fat coconut milk

1 ½ tbsp (22 ml) instant freeze-dried coffee (optional)

¼ tsp salt

1 tsp agar agar powder (see note)

15–20 vegan marshmallows, halved (see note)

Break apart the graham crackers and place them in a food processor. Process until very finely ground, about 1 to 2 minutes.

Place the chocolate chips and butter for the crust in a small microwave-safe bowl and zap for 30 seconds on high. Remove from microwave, whisk together until the chocolate is melted and add to the food processor along with the remaining crust ingredients. Process until the dates are incorporated and very well combined, about 3 minutes.

Transfer the dough to a 9-inch (23-cm) tart pan with a removable base coated with a nonstick cooking spray. Press with your fingers to form the crust, until it evenly coats the base and sides of the pan.

Place all of the filling ingredients into a small saucepan and heat over medium-low just until the chocolate chips are melted. Pour into the crust and place back in the fridge on an even surface.

While the pie chills, slice the marshmallows in half, then arrange on top of the pie. Place the top rack in the oven at its highest setting and place the pie on the rack. Broil (not bake!) for about 5–7 minutes, or until the marshmallows are golden brown, checking every minute to ensure they don't burn. Alternatively you can use a torch if you're super fancy.

Remove from the oven and place in the fridge. The pie shouldn't be warm at all, although the marshmallow is toasted. Cover loosely with plastic wrap and allow to chill for at least 2 hours prior to serving. Keep refrigerated.

notes: Full disclosure here: This is the only recipe in the book where I actually *smuggle* ingredients into Alaska from the States. Vegan marshmallows can be found at Whole Foods Market.

The agar agar powder could be omitted, but the pie will take longer to set. 1 tablespoon (5 g) of agar agar flakes can be used in place of the agar agar powder.

divine banana cream pie

Banana cream pie is one of my oldest BFFs in the realm of desserts. We share a long history together and I always feel a bit nostalgic when I think of that creamy, cold, custardy goodness. My mother is an awesome baker and for my birthdays, as a child, I was granted the opportunity to pick any celebratory cake or pie of my fancy and she would make it for me. My usual request was for, you guessed it, *banana cream pie.*

This Divine Banana Cream Pie was inspired after watching an episode of *The Mind of a Chef* where Christina from Momofuku Milk Bar made an unbelievable banana cream pie and it inspired me to make a vegan version. This is my *vegan* banana cream pie. I won't pretend it's not a bit fussy here and there. However, I assure you that the obnoxious little details are absolutely integral and once you taste the pie, you'll realize the fuss was definitely worth it!

makes 1 (9-inch [23-cm]) pie

Crust

½ cup (113 g) vegan granulated sugar

⅔ cup (120 g) all-purpose flour

⅔ cup (57 g) unsweetened cocoa powder

1 tsp cornstarch

½ tsp table salt

¼ cup (49 g) unrefined coconut oil, solid

2 tbsp (30 ml) water

Filling

2 medium (275 g) super-ripe black bananas, peeled

1 (13.6-oz [403-ml]) can of full-fat coconut milk, refrigerated overnight and divided

½ cup (113 g) vegan granulated sugar

¼ cup (79 g) raw cashews

2 tbsp (19 g) cornstarch

2 ½ tsp (9 g) agar agar powder (see note)

1 tsp vanilla extract

1 tsp ground turmeric (optional)

¼ tsp maple extract (optional)

½ tsp xanthan gum

1 cup (137 g) vegan powdered sugar

1 medium (137 g) ripe spotted banana, peeled and sliced

Preheat the oven to 300°F (150°C). Pulse 1 cup (226 g) of vegan granulated sugar in the food processor until finely ground. If you skip this step, you'll have a grainy pie. To make the crust, whisk together the dry crust ingredients, including ½ cup (113 g) of the finely ground sugar in a large mixing bowl. Melt the coconut oil in the microwave for 30 seconds and add it to the dry ingredients along with the water. Stir with a wooden spoon for 2 minutes, until the crumbled mixture resembles large peas.

Spread the mixture onto a large baking sheet lined with parchment paper or silpat. Bake for about 20 minutes or until it's dry to the touch. Remove from the oven and allow to cool slightly. Transfer to a 9-inch (23-cm) tart pan with a removable base coated with a nonstick cooking spray. Press with your fingers to form the crust, until it evenly coats the base and sides of the pan. Place in the fridge until ready to use.

To make the filling, add the black bananas to the blender. Open the chilled can of full-fat coconut milk and poke a hole in the cream so the milk can run out. Add ⅔ cup (160 ml) of the coconut milk (not the cream part) to the blender and place the can back in the fridge. Blend on high until smooth. Add in the remaining ½ cup (113 g) of finely processed vegan sugar and the remaining filling ingredients. Blend on high until completely smooth, transfer to a medium bowl and place in fridge until ready to use.

Add the remaining coconut milk and cream from the can, about ¾ cup (180 ml) to an electric mixer fixed with the whisk attachment. Whisk at medium-low speed, while slowly adding in the powdered sugar. Bring the speed to high and continue to whisk for about 5 minutes, until soft peaks have formed.

Whisk the chilled banana filling into the cream mixture on low speed until completely incorporated. Pour half of the filling into the chilled crust. Arrange the sliced banana in an even layer on top, then top with the remaining filling. Cover with plastic wrap and refrigerate for at least two hours, until completely chilled and set.

notes: Agar agar powder is not the same as the agar agar flakes. If you're using the flakes, change the amount to 5 tablespoons (25 g). However, unlike the powder, the flakes might not result in an ultra-smooth texture. I order my agar agar powder online.

If you don't have a tart pan, the crust will fit in a pie dish, but it will have to be spread pretty thin. It may also be a bit more difficult to serve out of a pie dish.

nutrition-rich brownies

Sometimes I *really* crave a brownie but want to avoid all the sugar, oil and flour. I still yearn for a rich, dense brownie full of deep chocolate flavor, but I need it to be healthy. You know what I mean? Some might say it's a contradiction, but not for me. I've developed a brownie solely for the days I'm looking to be *good* about being *bad*.

Blended walnuts and flax lend richness and help bind these brownies, while dates and beets (*yes, beets!*) sweeten it to perfection. Pulverized oats make an awesome substitute for regular ol' flour. Cocoa powder and instant coffee help to enhance the profound chocolate flavor along with a small helping of semi-sweet chocolate chips, the only nonwhole food ingredient! These brownies do have a *faint* beet flavor, so if you have an aversion to earthy beets, applesauce might do the trick.

These will never replace the classic, sugar and butter laden brownies in my life, but they're a great addition to a well-rounded dessert repertoire . . . *especially* when you're aiming to find yourself on the healthier side of sweet treats.

serves 9

3 tbsp (20 g) ground flaxseed

¼ cup + 2 tbsp (90 ml) water

2 (380 g) beets, chopped (see note)

2 tbsp (30 ml) water

1 cup (100 g) old-fashioned oats, dry

¼ cup (27 g) chopped walnuts

6 (100 g) medjool dates, pitted (see note)

¾ cup (140 g) semi-sweet, vegan chocolate chips

¼ cup (22 g) unsweetened cocoa powder

½ tbsp (9 g) instant coffee (optional, see note)

1 tsp vanilla extract

¼ tsp table salt

In a small bowl, whisk together the flax and ¼ cup + 2 tablespoons (90 ml) water. Allow to rest for about 15 minutes, or until ready to use.

Trim off the stem and tail of the beets; peel, then dice. Discard the peels. Add the diced beets to a microwave safe bowl along with the 2 tablespoons (30 ml) of water. Microwave on high for about 10 to 12 minutes, until fork-tender. I like to put a paper towel under the bowl as sometimes the water can boil over. Alternatively, if you don't use a microwave, the beets can be steamed in a rice cooker or over the stove until tender.

While the beets steam, add the oats to a food processor and process until they become the texture of flour, about 1 minute. Next, add in the walnuts and dates; pulverize into a paste, about 2 minutes.

Preheat the oven to 350°F (176°C). When the beets are done steaming, drain off the water and add the beets to the food processor along with the remaining ingredients. Process for good 3 to 5 minutes, until the entire mixture is very smooth. It should render into a thick paste.

Coat an 8 x 8-inch (20 x 20-cm) square baking dish with a nonstick cooking spray and spoon the batter into the dish. Using a spatula, even out the top of the batter. Bake for 25 minutes, until set. Cool completely on a wire cooling rack before slicing into 9 squares.

notes: I recommend using golden beets in this recipe because they don't stain quite as badly as the red variety and they're also milder in taste. However, red beets will work too.

If your dates are a little old and aren't very soft anymore, cover them with boiling water and soak the dates for about 10 minutes. Drain well prior to blending. Medjool dates can be found at your local grocery store and Costco.

The addition of instant coffee is optional, but it really helps bring out a deeper chocolate richness in baked goods. I like to keep a small jar on hand just for baking!

mulled berry galette

Galettes are the easier but somehow more awe-inspiring, lazier cousin of pie. If you hate making pie crusts (like me) and you always seem to abandon the handle bit of a piece of pie (like me), the galette is for you. It's pretty much foolproof.

This beautiful, rustic galette is stuffed with warm mixed berries that are gently mulled with comforting spices and refreshing lemon. This coconut-oil crust is simple to master as well! My favorite part about galettes? The uglier the better, as the more rustic it will look. No need for perfection here. You'll wow your friends and family, and they'll never know how easy it was to make!

serves 8

Berries

4 cups (471 g) frozen mixed berries

¼ cup (26 g) vegan granulated sugar

1 cinnamon stick, whole (or a dash of ground cinnamon)

⅛ tsp ground nutmeg

⅛ tsp ground cloves

1 tsp fresh lemon zest

2 tbsp (30 g) fresh lemon juice

½ tsp vanilla extract

2 tbsp (30 g) cornstarch

2 tbsp (30 ml) cold water

Dough

5 tbsp (75 ml) cold water

1 ¼ cups (163 g) all-purpose flour

1 tbsp (13 g) vegan granulated sugar

¼ tsp table salt

¼ cup (53 g) unrefined coconut oil, softened (room-temperature)

Finish

1 tsp unrefined coconut oil, softened (room-temperature)

½ tbsp (7 g) vegan granulated sugar

In a small saucepan, add the frozen berries, sugar and spices. Heat over medium-low for about 15 minutes, stirring occasionally, while preparing the dough. Be careful to not smash the berries too much. Here, we're looking to mull the berries and evaporate some of their liquid. Once the time is up, reduce the heat to low.

To make the dough, place the cold water in the freezer. Add the flour, sugar and salt to a food processor and pulse to combine. Then, while the processor is running, add the coconut oil 1 tablespoon (15 g) at a time. Process for about 1 minute, until the dough resembles a coarse meal with some larger chunks. Detach the processor bowl and place it in the freezer for 5 minutes (see note).

Once the 5 minutes is up, place the bowl back on the processor and with it running, drizzle in the cold water from the freezer. When pinched, the dough should stick together. If it crumbles, add more cold water, 1 tablespoon (15 ml) at a time.

Transfer the dough to a lightly floured surface and knead by hand about 6–8 times. Roll into a 13-inch (32.5-cm) circle, ensuring there are no holes. If you find a hole, patch it up. There should be no cracks, or the berry juice will run out when baked. Once rolled out, allow to rest for 10 minutes. Preheat the oven to 425°F (218°C).

While the dough rests stir the lemon zest, lemon juice and vanilla extract into the berry mixture. In a small bowl, whisk the cornstarch into the 2 tablespoons (30 ml) cold water. Then, whisk the cornstarch mixture into the berries. Stir gently until it's thickened slightly, about 1 minute. Remove from heat.

After the dough has rested, transfer it to a parchment-paper-lined baking sheet. Remove the cinnamon stick from the berries and transfer the mixture to the middle of the dough. Spread it out, until it's about 1 ½ inches (3.8 cm) from the edge of the dough; it's okay if the galette isn't perfectly circular. Fold the edges up over the berry mixture.

To finish, brush the top of the crust with coconut oil and sprinkle with sugar. Bake for 30 minutes, until the crust is slightly golden-brown and the berry juice is bubbling.

Allow to rest on a wire cooling rack for at least 10 to 15 minutes before serving. Slice into 9 pieces and serve warm.

note: I know it's kind of a pain but when making the dough, it's important to place the water and the bowl in the freezer. Everything must be kept chilled.

blueberry thyme lemon bars

Lemon bars are a favorite dessert of mine. However, I am *very* particular about them. I like them exceptionally tart and not cloyingly sweet. A more custardy bar is preferable to a cake-like one, in my book.

In my lemon bars, I love to use the wild blueberries that Todd and I pick in the fall and freeze to enjoy all year long. We pick them way up on a mountain ridge, in an area called Glacier View, where we got married. They lend the perfect complexity and sweetness to these tangy bars. The addition of thyme, baked into the buttery crust, offers the perfect bed for the vibrant pink filling. This dessert couldn't be easier to make, but it does require at least several hours in the fridge to set.

serves 6

Crust

1 cup (135 g) all-purpose flour

¼ cup (45 g) brown sugar

¼ cup (52 g) soft (room temperature) unrefined coconut oil

Zest from 1 lemon, about 1 tsp

½ tsp salt

¼ tsp dried thyme

2 tbsp (30 ml) water

Filling

Juice from 3 lemons, about ½ cup (120 ml)

¾ cup (150 g) vegan granulated sugar

¼ cup (30 g) all-purpose flour

¼ cup (85 g) agave nectar or maple syrup

⅔ cup (94 g) frozen wild blueberries (fresh could work as well)

½ tbsp (4 g) cornstarch

1 tsp agar agar powder or
1 tbsp (5 g) agar agar flakes

½ tsp vanilla extract

Preheat the oven to 350°F (176°C). In a large mixing bowl, stir together the crust ingredients. I like to use my electric stand mixer. When well combined, press into a 8 x 8-inch (20 x 20-cm) baking dish coated with a nonstick cooking spray. Bake the crust for about 20 minutes, until the edges are just turning golden brown. Remove from oven, place on a wire cooling rack and reduce the heat to 300°F (149°C).

While the crust bakes, add all the filling ingredients to a blender and blend on high for 1–2 minutes, until well combined and very smooth. Pour the filling into the baked crust. The crust does not need to be completely cooled. Bake for 25 minutes, until the middle doesn't jiggle much when given a little shake.

Allow to cool on a wire cooling rack at least 1 hour or until room temperature before covering with plastic wrap and placing in the fridge. Allow to rest overnight or several hours until completely set. It might look like it won't set up, but it will. The top will still look very glassy; however, the bars will hold their shape completely once cut.

Cut into 6 bars. Store in the fridge.

note: These bars are very easy to throw together, but they do take a while to set. It's best to allow them to rest overnight, if possible. They are worth the wait, trust me.

rye sugar cookies w/ salted chocolate rosemary glaze

While growing up, I mostly made completely plain and exceptionally *dull* cookies. The reason behind this is my father. He always requested "chocolate chip cookies without the chips." *What?* What is that?! That's just flour, sugar and butter! The plebeians of cookies, I should think.

I suspect it's because of this that, as an adult, I enjoy experimenting with all sorts of unique cookies. These crunchy rye sugar cookies are one of my fondest experiments. They almost remind me of shortbread and are the perfect coffee companion. The rye flour lends a bit of nuttiness, texture and an earthy appeal. Dipped in a rosemary-infused, dark chocolate glaze and topped with flake salt, these are complex in flavor and definitely a foodie's cookie.

makes 24 cookies

Cookies

2 tbsp (12 g) ground flaxseed

¼ cup (60 ml) cold water

1 ¼ cups (101 g) all-purpose flour

1 ¼ cups (157 g) dark rye flour (see note)

1 tsp baking powder

½ tsp table salt

1 cup (201 g) vegan granulated sugar

¾ cup (157 g) vegan stick butter, softened to room temperature

½ tbsp (7 ml) vanilla extract

Glaze

¼ cup (56 g) vegan stick butter

¼ cup (56 g) unrefined coconut oil

¾–1 cup (90-120 g) vegan powdered suger

¼ cup (17 g) unsweetened cocoa powder

½ tsp vanilla extract

½ tsp fresh rosemary, minced

Flake salt, for garnish

24 rosemary leaves, for garnish

Preheat oven to 375°F (190°C) and line a large baking sheet with parchment paper or silpat. In a small bowl, whisk together the flax and water. Place in fridge and allow to rest until ready to use.

In a large mixing bowl, whisk together the flours, baking powder and salt. Set aside.

In an electric mixing bowl, add the sugar, butter and vanilla. Beat on medium-high speed until somewhat light and fluffy, about 3 to 5 minutes. Reduce the speed to low and beat in the flax mixture. While the mixer is running, slowly add in the flour mixture. Mix on low until just combined.

Roll about 1 tablespoon (18 g) of the dough into a ball and place on the baking sheet. Repeat until there are 12 cookies on the baking sheet. Place the remaining dough in the fridge until ready to use. Flatten each cookie to about ½ inch (1.3 cm) thick with the bottom of a glass. They should be about 2 inches (5 cm) in diameter. Keep them at least 1 inch (2.5 cm) apart. Bake for 12 to 15 minutes, until the edges just begin to turn golden brown. Remove from the oven and carefully transfer the cookies to a wire cooling rack. Repeat with remaining dough.

Wait until the second batch of cookies is completely cool before making the glaze. To make the glaze, melt the butter and coconut oil in a medium, microwave-safe bowl. Whisk in the remaining ingredients and beat vigorously for about 2 minutes until there are no remaining sugar clumps. The glaze should be glossy and completely smooth.

Dip the cookies face first into the glaze, then place back on the wire cooling rack. Add a dash of flake salt and press one rosemary leaf on top of each cookie. Allow the glaze to set on the cookies overnight or several hours. When storing, keep cool.

notes: Light rye flour, whole wheat flour or additional all-purpose flour can be used in place of the dark rye flour.

Add a bit more powdered sugar if the glaze seems runny and a splash of vegan milk if it seems a bit thick. The cookies can be eaten with the glaze soft or hardened. It won't harden up completely like a shell, but enough so that the cookies can be stacked and stored. If you prefer the glaze very hard, they can be stored in the fridge.

cappuccino meringues

Is there anything chickpeas can't do? They benevolently gift us hummus, socca and falafel to name just a few recipes, an absolutely *marvelous* little legume, indeed. I confess to buying them canned because I never know when the little MVPs will need to make a surprise appearance and it's wonderful to have them cooked and ready. Best yet, the darlings have bestowed upon us . . . *meringue.* Yes, meringue. Sing it from the heavens, people! A meringue, that I *promise,* does not taste in the least like beans and is 100% as fluffy and crispy as regular ol' egg-white meringues. *Omnivore verified.* I first made vegan meringues for my mom on Mother's Day. They are one of her favorite desserts and she gave them the bonafide meringue-loving, mom-stamp-of-approval.

She couldn't believe I made them out of the water from a can of chickpeas that one usually drains down the sink! These vegan meringues will straight-up *blow your mind.* They are crispy, crunchy and taste of sweet creamy coffee. A perfect breakfast treat or dessert!

makes about 24 meringues

⅔ cup (160 ml) canned chickpea water (from one 15.5-oz [439-g] can of chickpeas)

¾ cup (174 g) vegan granulated sugar

2 tbsp (8 g) instant, freeze-dried coffee (see note)

1 tsp vanilla extract

½ tsp cream of tartar, white vinegar or lemon juice

Preheat the oven to 215°F (101°C).

Add the chickpea water to an electric stand mixer assembled with the whisk attachment. Beat on high for about 2 minutes until foamy and thick, then slowly add in the sugar while the mixer is still running. Beat on high for about 2 to 5 additional minutes or until the mixture becomes very thick, white and glossy.

While the mixer is still running, add in the coffee, vanilla and cream of tartar. Beat to combine until the coffee has been dissolved, about 1 to 2 minutes, and the meringue holds a stiff peak.

Using a spoon, dollop golf-ball-sized meringues onto two parchment lined baking sheets. They won't spread too much, so they can be spaced about 1 inch (2.5 cm) apart.

Bake for about 1 hour and 20 minutes, until matte. They should no longer be glossy and should lift off the pan fairly easily using your fingers. At this point there are three options, depending on how much time you have, which are listed below. Option 1 is the most ideal and recommended.

1. Once done baking, turn off the oven and allow the meringues to cool in the oven overnight with the door shut.
2. Turn off the oven and allow the meringues to rest in the oven with the door shut for at least 30 minutes to 1 hour; then allow them to cool at room temperature, ideally on the pan.
3. Turn off the oven and allow them to cool at room temperature, ideally on the pan.

Store the meringues in an airtight container with a few silica gel packets—do not eat these, and store away from children! The silica packets, the little guys that come in your vitamins bottles and electronic packages, will help keep the meringues moisture-free.

notes: I don't recommend making meringues on a rainy or high-humidity day. They will become chewy instead of crunchy, but I don't mind them a bit chewy at all.

These are *super-duper* coffee flavored. If you'd prefer a subtler coffee flavor, use just 1 tablespoon (4 g) of instant coffee.

german chocolate cups

German chocolate cake. The only birthday dessert accepted (nay, assumed) by my dad, brothers and grandpa. Chocolate, coconut and pecans run strong in the blood of the men in my family. It's not even in the cards to attempt to make any of them anything else. Needless to say there is *a lot* of German chocolate cake baking and eating throughout the year.

Well finally . . . I'd had enough! It was time for something different. However, I knew it wouldn't be prudent to stray *too* far from our mores. Last year I timidly decided to make German chocolate cupcakes—not too much of a deviation (they are delicious and on the blog). *A hit!*

Straying a little bit further from the usual, I thought I'd make German chocolate cups. Personally, I'd eat 'em all day long over german chocolate cake. They come together in about 15 minutes, which is much less time than it takes to make a three-tiered cake. If you have 15 minutes, you, too, can make these chocolate cups. They're super-easy and I imagine would be a lot of fun for kids to help with!

makes 12 cups

1 ¼ cups (227 g) vegan semi-sweet chocolate chips

½ cup (122 g) plain, unsweetened nondairy milk

4 (64 g) medjool dates, pitted and rough chopped

1 tsp vanilla extract

½ cup (68 g) vegan powdered sugar

½ cup (50 g) shredded coconut flakes

¼ cup (27 g) pecans, chopped

Fill a medium saucepan or pot with water. Place a medium heat-safe bowl (I use a glass Pyrex one) on top and increase or decrease the water so that it's about 1 inch (2.5 cm) below the bottom of the heat-safe bowl.

Bring the water to a boil over high heat (with the heat-safe bowl removed). Once boiling, reduce to a simmer and place the bowl on top. Add the chocolate chips to the bowl and whisk continually until just melted, about 4 minutes. Turn off the heat and remove the bowl from above the saucepan; set aside.

While the water is boiling, place the milk, dates and vanilla extract into a food processor or blender. Process until very smooth and creamy, about 3 minutes, scraping down the sides as needed. Next, add in the powdered sugar, coconut flakes and pecans. Process until just combined and set aside until the chocolate is ready.

Place 12 paper or silicone muffin liners into a muffin pan. Place ½ tablespoon (7 ml) of melted chocolate in one of the liners and tilt it around in a circle to coat the edges a bit. Next, add in 1 tablespoon (6 g) of the coconut filling and smoosh gently with the back of the tablespoon. Follow with one more ½ tablespoon (7 ml) layer of melted chocolate. Tilt the cup so the chocolate covers the top and sides of the filling. Repeat with the remaining chocolate and filling.

Place in the fridge for about 30 minutes to harden. Serve chilled. Store in an airtight container in the fridge, the freezer or at room temperature.

white russian tiramisu

I might live in Wasilla with Sarah Palin but that doesn't mean I can see Russia from my house. However, I can make this White Russian Tiramisu. It's actually very dear to me, as tiramisu is my absolutely *favorite* dessert. I remember making this tiramisu often with my mother and how she taught me the correct way to dip the ladyfingers so that they don't end up a soggy mess. However, I've developed an airy vegan cake made with a vegan meringue that can stand up to being dipped in coffee, creating a cruelty-free spin on this classic tiramisu.

Similar to my White Wine "Clam" Linguine (page 97), I avoided making this holy grail of a dessert for a long time out of fear that it wouldn't live up to my expectations nor my fervent nostalgia. After many, many attempts and a few tiramisu-related breakdowns, I finally perfected the recipe! It's with abundant joy that I'm at long last able to share this exceptionally special dessert with you. My nonvegan friends totally raved about this tiramisu and I know you will, too!

serves 8

Cake

½ cup (60 ml) chickpea water—the liquid from 1 (15.5-oz [439-g]) can of chickpeas

½ tsp cream of tartar, lemon juice or white vinegar

⅔ cup (160 g) vegan granulated sugar

½ tsp vanilla extract

1 cup (121 g) all-purpose flour

1 tsp baking powder

Dash of table salt

Filling

8 oz (227 g) + ½ cup (116 g) vegan cream cheese (I like Tofutti)

3 tbsp (45 ml) Kahlua, divided

⅓ cup (74 g) vegan brown sugar

⅓ cup (82 g) vegan powdered (icing or confectioner's) sugar

1 tbsp (15 ml) melted unrefined coconut oil

2 tsp (6 g) cornstarch

½ tsp xanthan gum (optional)

¾ cup (180 ml) double-strength, strongly brewed coffee (I like to make it with instant coffee)

2 tsp (3 g) unsweetened cocoa powder, divided

Preheat the oven to 375°F (190°C) and line a 8 ½ x 4 ½-inch (21.6 x 11.4-cm) bread pan with parchment paper. Don't skip this step!

Add the chickpea water and cream of tartar to an electric stand mixing bowl. Using the whisk attachment, beat for about 3 to 5 minutes until very white, foamy and thick. Slowly add in the sugar and vanilla and beat for about 5 more minutes until the meringue is glossy and forms stiff peaks.

In a medium mixing bowl, whisk together the flour, baking powder and salt. Slowly fold the flour mixture into the meringue with a wooden spoon until just combined. Pour the batter into the lined bread pan and use the back of the spoon to even out the top. Bake for about 20 minutes, until the top is a dark golden-brown all over. The middle will sink a bit and that's okay. Remove the cake from the oven, allow to rest for about 5 minutes in the pan, then carefully flip it upside down onto a wire cooling rack. Remove the parchment paper and allow the cake to rest until completely cool, about 1–2 hours; this is important, or it will be very difficult to slice. Throw away the parchment paper and keep the pan handy.

While the cake bakes, clean out the electric mixing bowl. Add the cream cheese and 2 tablespoons (30 ml) of Kahlua; beat on low speed until just combined. Be careful not to overbeat the cream cheese or it will become runny. Now, slowly beat in the sugars. Once combined, beat in the coconut oil. Sift in the cornstarch and xanthan gum and beat until just combined. Cover and place in the fridge until ready to use.

Add the coffee and 1 tablespoon (15 ml) Kahlua to a large plate. Place the bread pan close by. When the cake is completely cool, cut it in half lengthwise with a serrated knife. Quickly dip both sides of one of the cake halves into the coffee mixture. It should soak up liquid, but not so much that it falls apart when you lift it out. Place it on the bottom of the bread pan. If it breaks apart a little, that's okay. Evenly spread half the cream cheese filling over the dipped cake and sift 1 teaspoon of unsweetened cocoa powder over the filling. Repeat with the other half of the dipped cake, filling and cocoa powder.

Cover and chill completely, about 2 hours, until the filling is mostly set. Cut into 8 squares and serve chilled.

cardamom-spiced nectarine cupcakes w/ fluffy meringue

Cardamom, my favorite spice, makes an exceptional companion for the nectarine, which coincidentally is my favorite fruit! Thus, I often find myself eagerly developing new recipes in which I'm able to marry the two darlings. Sweet fruit topped with a dreamy meringue is a humble, yet profoundly scrumptious sweet treat. It was a small stroke of genius when I decided to tie the two together in a moist, vanilla cupcake. This dessert is really the best of everything: cake, fruit and meringue! It should be noted that these are best consumed the same day.

makes 12 cupcakes

Dry

1 ²/₃ cups (211 g) all-purpose flour

1 cup (190 g) vegan granulated sugar

1 tsp baking powder

¾ tsp ground cardamom

¼ tsp baking soda

¼ tsp table salt

Wet

¾ cup (170 g) vegan stick butter, room temperature

½ cup (120 ml) chickpea water—a portion of the liquid from 1 (15.5-oz [439-g]) can of chickpeas (see note)

1 tbsp (15 ml) vanilla extract

½ cup (120 g) vegan sour cream

½ cup (120 ml) plain, unsweetened nondairy milk

Meringue

¼ cup (60 ml) chickpea water—the remaining liquid from the previously opened can of chickpeas

¼ tsp xanthan gum (optional, see note)

¹/₈ tsp cream of tartar, lemon juice or white vinegar

¼ cup (48 g) vegan granulated sugar

1 tsp vanilla extract

3 small (180 g) nectarines or peaches, divided

Whisk the dry ingredients together in a large electric mixing bowl. Then, with the flat beater attachment, beat the wet ingredients one at a time into the dry until incorporated. Do not overbeat.

Prepare a regular cupcake pan with silicone or paper liners and preheat the oven to 350°F (177°C). Finely dice 2 of the nectarines. To fill the cupcake liners, add ½ heaping tablespoon (9 ml) of batter into one liner, scatter in 1 teaspoon of diced nectarines, then finish with 1 heaping tablespoon (17 ml) of batter. The liners should be almost completely filled. Repeat with remaining liners. Bake for 25 minutes, until the tops are golden brown. Clean out the mixing bowl very well.

Turn out the cupcakes from the pan once done cooking and allow to rest on a wire cooling rack until completely cool, about 1 hour. Make the meringue only when the cupcakes are cool. Cut the remaining nectarine into 12 slices and set aside.

To make the meringue, add the chickpea water, xanthan gum and cream of tartar to a large electric mixing bowl with the whisk attachment. It will seem like too little for the bowl, but I assure you it will be okay. Whisk on medium for about 1 minute, then increase the speed to high and whisk for an additional 2–3 minutes until the liquid turns white and fluffy. With the machine running, add in the sugar and vanilla. Whisk for about 5 to 7 additional minutes until it's very fluffy, sticky and holds a stiff peak. If you turn the bowl upside down the meringue should stay in place.

Transfer the meringue into a small Ziploc bag (or piping bag if you're fancy) and close the end. Cut a ¾ inch (19 mm) wide slice off one of the bottom corners of the bag. Pipe the meringue onto the cupcakes and top with a slice of nectarine.

These cupcakes don't store well because of the meringue. If there are leftovers, the meringue will turn foamy but still hold its shape and taste fine. I suggest using a different frosting if these won't be shared and eaten in the same day.

notes: If you've never made chickpea meringue before, you're in for a real treat. All you need is one can of chickpeas; try to get the unsalted variety. Just drain the chickpeas and reserve the liquid from the can. There should be about ½–¾ cup (120–180 ml) of liquid. If you have a little extra, add it to soup or a smoothie for a protein boost! Use the chickpeas in any number of the recipes containing chickpeas in this book!

You can leave the xanthan gum out, but the meringue won't be quite as sturdy.

drinks

refreshing concoctions and nutritious smoothies

Need something to quench that thirst? You've come to the right place, as I happen to have a few tantalizing options for you. If you're looking for something *super-refreshing*, a little sweet and tart with a hint of herbal essence, then my Sparkling Rosemary Grapefruitade (page 192) is absolutely perfect. There are also a couple of good and healthy smoothie recipes that are great for breakfast or just a quick snack. Smoothies are a fantastic way to get in some healthy fats like flaxseed and/or avocado, while filling up on nutritious fruit, helping to keep sugar cravings at bay.

You'll also find a recipe for one of my favorite beverages. It's an obscure little drink, known as shrub (see page 196); the recipe passed down from my grandparents. Shrub is a fermented, sugary, vinegary syrup that's mixed with water and crushed ice for a fresh, mouth-puckering beverage that reminds me of my childhood. Just like smoothies, it's a delicious way to use up any excess fruit from the harvest . . . or forlorn fruit left over from a farmer's market bonanza.

sparkling rosemary grapefruitade

There's only one way I enjoy grapefruit: *juiced.* It's just a tad too bitter for my delicate little tastebuds. Grapefruit *juice,* however, makes them sing with joy! One day I pulled a couple of these large fellas out of my CSA, wrinkling up my nose at them and wondering what to do with the bad boys. Spring was emerging and I had just bought a budding rosemary plant. That's when the idea popped into my head to create a rosemary and grapefruit flavored nod to soda (or "pop," if you're from the Midwest).

I regularly consume what we, in my family, call *fuzzy water*—a.k.a. sparkling water. Todd and I received a SodaStream a few years ago as a gift and use it every day to make plain, sparkling water. On special occasions it's a lot of fun to mix with homemade syrups from berries and herbs or my Vintage Strawberry-Basil Shrub (page 196)!

serves 2

1 large (518 g) ruby red grapefruit, juiced

1 medium (89 g) lemon, juiced

2 tbsp (30 ml) agave nectar or maple syrup

¼–½ tsp fresh rosemary, minced

8 ice cubes

1 cup (240 ml) sparkling water, to taste, divided

Juice the grapefruit and lemon into a large Mason jar or glass. The grapefruit should provide about 1 cup (240 ml) of juice and the lemon about ¼ cup (60 ml) of juice.

Whisk in the agave nectar and rosemary. Allow to rest for about 5 minutes so that the rosemary can infuse the juice. Strain into a separate liquid measuring cup or Mason jar using a fine mesh strainer.

Divide the ice cubes between two drinking glasses and pour half the juice into each glass. Top each glass with ½ cup (120 ml) of sparkling water; stir gently to combine.

Serve cold.

note: Stir in additional sparkling water if you'd prefer the flavor a bit muted.

french toast smoothie

This is a favorite on the blog and I was blown away by all the comments of readers exclaiming how much they loved it! You'll be shocked at how perfectly this somewhat peculiar smoothie tastes *just like* French toast! This smoothie is the *ultimate* breakfast; super quick, delicious, nutritious, sweet and light. Some of the ingredients might seem odd, but I assure you this is the real deal!

Grab your blender and salute that perfect combination of egg, maple syrup and sweet vanilla that's usually reserved only for actual French toast. Sometimes you just don't want to go to the trouble to make a proper breakfast: *Enter this smoothie.*

serves 1

1 cup (240 ml) plain, unsweetened soymilk (see note)

¼ medium (51 g) avocado, chopped and frozen

½ tbsp (4 g) large-flake nutritional yeast (see note)

1 ½ tbsp (22 ml) real maple syrup

½ tsp ground flaxseed

½ tsp vanilla extract

¼ tsp ground cinnamon

Dash of freshly grated nutmeg

Pinch of salt

Add all the ingredients to a blender and blend on high until smooth and creamy. Pour into a chilled glass and serve cold.

notes: I like to use soymilk in this recipe. Almond milk and coconut milk are a little too strongly flavored for this delicate smoothie.

The nutritional yeast is essential for this recipe, so don't leave it out!

This recipe easily scales for a crowd.

vintage strawberry-basil shrub

Do you *enjoy* the taste of vinegar? Consider yourself an *old soul*? Have an unmanageable quantity of fruit from your garden? Is your grandmother your idol? All these questions must be asked before embarking on the very sacred art of shrub making. If you're thinking I'm about to give you a recipe for edible hedge clippings, you are mistaken. "Shrub" is a drinking vinegar. It's basically a syrupy fruit vinegar that's made from equal parts fruit, sugar and vinegar. The sugar and fruit ferment while it rests in the fridge. It was (and still is) a great way to use excess fruit, as it keeps for the better part of a year. The syrup is diluted, to taste, with water or sparkling water. If you enjoy kombucha, you'll probably enjoy shrub.

My grandparents always made *raspberry* shrub. They had vast rows upon rows of huge, plump raspberries. Their recipe was handed down from my grandmother on a yellow, tattered piece of paper torn from a notebook. I've been making my own shrub for several years. It's a refreshing and healthy fruit drink to be enjoyed all year long and I love to experiment with different fruit, floral and herbal essences. This strawberry and basil shrub version is my favorite.

makes 32 oz (946 ml)

3 cups (662 g) fresh strawberries, diced

3 cups (438 g) vegan granulated sugar

¼ cup (14 g) fresh basil, minced

3 cups (700 ml) apple cider vinegar

Crushed ice (for serving)

Combine the strawberries, sugar and minced basil in a large mixing bowl. Mix together with clean hands, mashing the strawberries between your fingers. Be sure to really incorporate the sugar into the berries; it will end up a wet mess. This is important! It will take about 5 minutes to massage the berries; I like to think of it like a sort of meditation. There shouldn't be any dry sugar remaining.

Cover the bowl and place in the fridge to rest for 24 to 72 hours. After a time, the strawberries should be surrounded by a watery liquid and bubbles should start to form.

After the mixture has rested, strain out the liquid into a small bowl using a fine mesh strainer. Use a ladle to scoop out any remaining strawberries from the bowl, leaving the sugar undisturbed. Try to avoid scraping up the leftover sugar at the bottom of the bowl. Use the back of a wooden spoon to press the berries into the strainer to extract as much liquid as possible. Add the strained juice back to the mixing bowl and whisk it into the sugar along with the vinegar until the sugar is dissolved. Bag and freeze the strawberries for use in pie or smoothies, you won't need them for the shrub any longer.

Transfer the sugary liquid to grolsch-style bottles (also called flip-top or swing-top bottles, see note) using a funnel. Cap and store in the fridge for at least 1 week or up to 8 months. The flavors meld together and the vinegary tang mellows as the shrub is permitted to age.

To serve, shake the bottle well and pour a bit of shrub into a glass filled with crushed ice. Dilute with plain or sparkling water to taste and stir. I use about 1 part shrub to 5 parts water. Ice is non-negotiable, and I say this as an anti-ice person! Use crushed as opposed to cubes if you can get your hands on it (I don't deny snagging crushed ice from the gym and/or work and toting it home). If you fancy it, shrub can also be mixed into cocktails in place of bitters.

notes: Almost any fruit can be used in place of the strawberries. Feel free to play around!

You can find grolsch-style bottles online at Amazon.com, specialty kitchen stores or beer equipment stores. Also, some beer from the liquor store actually comes in this type of bottles. Drink the beer and save the bottle to make shrub! It's a win-win.

green tea & berry smoothie

This is one of my favorite invigorating smoothies. With its creamy berry and green tea flavors, healthy flaxseed and antioxidant-rich cinnamon, it keeps my body nourished. Matcha is made from new green tea leaves that are dried and pulverized into a powder. It comes in several different quality grades but for baking and smoothies, it's practical to use a culinary grade matcha.

I make this often as a pre-dinner snack or a super quick breakfast on the go. Sometimes I'll double the recipe and bring it to work in a tall Mason jar if I didn't have time to pack a lunch!

serves 2

1 cup (240 ml) plain, unsweetened nondairy milk

1 cup (67 g) frozen mixed berries

½ medium (66 g) banana, sliced

1 tsp matcha, culinary grade or 1 tsp loose-leaf green tea (see note)

½ tsp ground flaxseed

¼ tsp ground cinnamon

Place all the ingredients in a blender and whiz on high until creamy and smooth. Serve cold.

note: Matcha can be found online at Amazon.com, in Asian markets or in the tea section of your local grocery store in small tubs. Feel free to use loose-leaf green tea if you can't find matcha. Just throw the leaves right in the blender!

quick tips on reducing food waste

The most helpful thing one can do to reduce food waste is clearly to only buy as much perishable food as one will use. Excess food means some of it occasionally gets pushed to the back of the fridge or buried under newer produce. In addition, the longer fruits and vegetables sit, the more nutrients they lose. Fresh is best!

To avoid wasting food and to consume the freshest fruits and vegetables possible, this usually means more frequent trips to the farmer's market and/or grocery store. But it doesn't have to! I participate in a CSA (community supported agriculture) cooperative that delivers a box that's filled with Northwestern- and Alaskan-grown produce. I pick it up once a week on my way home from work. Sometimes CSAs offer varying sizes of boxes and several pickup locations. I can even hold deliveries if I am on vacation. Check out your state's CSA list online to find out more information about joining one.

As vegans, Todd and I eat mostly fruits and veggies and so joining a CSA has cut down on our grocery store trips almost entirely. The best part is that we use up pretty much all the produce within that one week, eating it at its prime. If I do have any stragglers at the end of the week when my new box is due, I make smoothies or a vegetable soup. It's a great way to avoid tossing out overripe fruit or wrinkled potatoes.

When buying perishables for the week, it's helpful to use the most delicate in the beginning of the week. When I get asparagus, spinach, herbs, tomatoes and so on, I try to use them up first. I cut the leaves off the beets the day they arrive and sauté them as a side dish for dinner that evening! After the most perishable vegetables have been used, I move on to the more hearty guys like cabbage, potatoes, carrots and more.

On the following page, you'll find a short but detailed bit of information on how to avoid wasting food with regard to specific food items.

VEGETABLES

I usually lean toward not peeling vegetables. Not only is this the lazy lady's approach to cooking, but it's also the healthier and more environmentally friendly approach. Many nutrients and fiber are found in the peel and there's also no peel scraps to discard this way.

Most of my vegetable scraps (carrot tops, onion cores, zucchini tops, etc.) go into a large, plastic freezer bag. When the bag is full, I make a stock out of the scraps in my pressure cooker. I have a recipe for the stock on my blog at www.produceonparade.com. I even throw in pumpkin rinds, garlic paper and all sorts of crazy stuff. I think it's important to note that the scraps should be washed well and organic, if possible. If in doubt, compost!

Some scraps, like kale, broccoli, chard, cabbage, brussels sprouts, mustard greens and pretty much any cruciferous vegetable shouldn't go into the stock, because they can turn it bitter. I chop these up into bite-size pieces and put them in a separate freezer container. They go into my dog's toy, which can be stuffed with treats. Never give your dog garlic or onions (these should be in the stock, anyway)!

My favorite way to use leftover avocado is to smash it up on toast and then top with nutritional yeast.

This is how I manage to use almost all of my vegetable scraps!

HERBS

If you've got cilantro stems or other herb bits that you don't need in dishes, throw them into the stock baggie! I'll put them in smoothies too. If you've got a bunch of parsley that's wilted and sad, into the freezer stock bag it goes!

I love growing my own herbs in the summer. I save money and I just clip off as much as needed! Herbs can be kept over winter in pots, too, or just have a few on the windowsill.

FRUITS

Fruit scraps can be composted. The greens of fruits, like strawberry tops, can go right into the blender for smoothies. No need to chop them off! If I find fruit that seems to be aging quickly I'll chop it up and throw in it a large, plastic freezer bag filled with scraps that I add to smoothies.

Bananas have their own, separate freezer bag. I peel them and break 'em in half before putting them in the bag. Have lemons and limes that need to be used up quickly? Squeeze the juice and make vinaigrette for a salad or add it to a glass of water. Aging tomatoes or tomato scraps can go into the stock baggie.

BEANS

Leftover canned beans (if I didn't use the entire can) can be thrown into smoothies for a protein boost or used as a topping for a salad.

acknowledgments

Page Street Publishing—Will and Sarah, if it weren't for your complete conviction in me, this cookbook wouldn't exist. You sought me out, instilled complete confidence in the fact that I could be an author and patiently guided me through the rigorous process of writing a cookbook, all the while cheering me on. Rarely has there been such an utter outpouring of complete faith! Your dedication and trust in your authors is something to be admired. I can't imagine working with anyone else. My champions, thank you.

My Recipe Testers—You were such an extraordinary help in the perfection of these recipes. Thank you for all your hard work and dedication. I'm forever indebted to you!

- Deanna Marsh
- Erin Kearns
- Janet Dery Cox
- Jeremy Kearns
- Kaitlyn Scalisi
- Kate Alber
- Marina Fabian
- Martha Brookbank
- Meredith Oakes
- Natalie M. Davidson
- Olivia Wall
- Perrine Bellanger
- Yoyo Andande

My Tasters—You know who you are. Your job wasn't that hard . . . in fact it was pretty great. Regardless, I still thank you for putting up with several batches of tiramisu and scones; thank you.

about the author

Katie is the writer, recipe developer, food stylist, photographer and creative mind behind the vegan food and lifestyle blog Produce On Parade. She was born and raised in rural Alaska where she lives with her husband, Todd, and dog, Bailey. They just completed their dream home at the back of seven wooded acres, in 2015. In this private sanctuary Katie enjoys running, yoga, gardening, painting and watching the chickadees. A mammographer by day and cook by night, her days are busy yet filled with love and good food.

index

Note: Page numbers in italics indicate photos.

D

E

F

G

P

Q

R

S

T

U

V

W

X

Z